THE STEAKHOUSE COOKBOOK

AUTHORS OF

The Chesapeake Bay Fish &
Fowl Cookbook

The Grand Central Oyster Bar &
Restaurant Seafood Cookbook

A Collection of the
Best Recipes from
the Great Steakhouses
of the U.S.

THE
STEAKHOUSE
COOKBOOK

By JOAN and JOE FOLEY

FREUNDLICH BOOKS   NEW YORK

The Colemans have always known what
a great steak is all about—and this
book is for them. . . .

Published by Freundlich Books
(A division of Lawrence Freundlich Publications, Inc.)
212 Fifth Avenue
New York, N.Y. 10010

Distributed to the trade by The Scribner Books Companies, Inc.
115 Fifth Avenue
New York, N.Y. 10003

Manufactured in the United States of America

10 9 8 7 6 5 4 3 2 1

Library of Congress Cataloging-in-Publication Data
Foley, Joan.
  The steakhouse cookbook.
  Includes index.
1. Cookery (Beef) 2. Cookery, American. 3. Menus.
I. Foley, Joe. II. Title.
TX749.F65 1985   641.5   85-27549
ISBN 0-88191-021-X

CONTENTS

** All recipes in this book are for
four persons unless otherwise specified.*

THE STEAKHOUSE COOKBOOK

WELCOME TO STEAKHOUSE U.S.A.

FOOD FADS and styles change as frequently as the weather, but steak is still America's favorite meal and the great steakhouses of the United States are an American tradition. This book is a celebration of that tradition.

There can be sawdust on the floor and long horns on the wall, or fine linens on the table and crystal chandeliers, but one thing all the best steakhouses have in common is expertly prepared and stylishly served top quality beef.

Dinner at a truly fine steakhouse is an event, and we're going to help you to create not only the spectacular meals but also some of that special steakhouse ambience in your own home.

You'll have unique access to the kitchens of these great steakhouses in a collection of recipes that have been put together just like a restaurant menu. Part of the fun is selecting your meal from the menu, appetizer to after-dinner mint, just as you would in a restaurant, and then preparing it to serve at home "steakhouse style" for family and friends.

Once you've selected the recipes you'll be serving, a hand-written menu will add to the festivity and anticipation of the meal. Use your imagination with paper, pen, drawings, and cut-outs in creating and "personalizing" this menu for your steakhouse at home. Distribute copies of the menu the day before the big dinner, or during cocktails the night of the meal. The menu will also serve as a nice memento if the occasion for the dinner is a special one, such as a birthday or an anniversary.

Just to get you started, and we know you'll have ideas of your own, your menu might look like this:

Fresh Jumbo Shrimp Cocktail
Cup of Home-Made Beef Bouillon
Boneless Sliced Sirloin Steak with Broiled Mushroom Caps
Oven-Roasted New Potatoes in Jackets   Green Peas with Mint
Sliced Beefsteak Tomatoes and Red Onions Vinaigrette
Corn Bread Squares with Home-made Sweet Butter
Coffee Rum Ice Cream
Old-Fashioned Hot Chocolate Fudge Sauce (Optional)

Restaurateurs have to be good showmen, and an important part of any steakhouse meal is how the food is presented. Ambience is important, too. If filet mignon is on the menu, dress up the table with a snowy white linen cloth and napkins. Get out the candlesticks and crystal, and of course your best dishes and silver. When you're serving a *big* steak, a double porterhouse or heavyweight sirloin for instance, a checkered tablecloth with matching dish towels for napkins fit right in with the mood of the food. With the emphasis on *big*, use individual and preferably white serving platters for each steak, and *big* bowls and *big* side dishes of everything! Just be sure there are no picky eaters at the table for this meal, although all the recipes in the book can do double duty as great leftovers. If you're carving beef at the table, have an attractive fork and carving knife set ready that you use just for this purpose.

Most steakhouse owners privately wince at the sight of a ketchup bottle, but what one puts on a steak is serious business for beef-lovers, even if it's only a sprinkling of freshly ground black pepper. These are the "add-ons" that are most often requested in steakhouses, and they should be served on a rolling tea cart or TV table that sits off to one side ready to be wheeled to the table as needed:

Ketchup	Small bowl of minced raw onion
A.1. Steak sauce	Small bowl of minced fresh garlic
Chili sauce	Salt
Worcestershire sauce	Pepper mill
Mustard	

The success of the steak dinner that no one ever forgets depends of course on *the beef*, and that means buying the very best quality meat you can find and cooking it to perfection. We talk *All About Beef* in another section of this book beginning on page 35.

Meanwhile, we'd like to convince you that dining at home can be almost as much fun as eating out—if you do it with "steakhouse" style!

Let's take a look at the menu ....

THE MENU

Appetizers

VEGETABLE JUICE COCKTAIL

Ten Garden-Fresh Vegetables Combined in a Home-Made Tomato Juice Cocktail : 19

JUMBO SHRIMP WITH COCKTAIL SAUCE

Plump Jumbo Shrimp in a Tangy Tomato Cocktail Sauce : 20

AVOCADO CUP WITH "HOUSE" FRENCH DRESSING

Avocado Cubes Tossed in a Special Sweet-and-Tart "House" French Dressing : 22

BROILED MELON SLICES

Ripe and Juicy Cantaloupe Slices Broiled with a Crusty Brown Sugar and Lemon and Lime Topping : 22

TOMATO ASPIC WITH WHIPPED LIME CREAM

A Light Tomato Gelatin Flecked with Onion and Celery and Topped with Whipped Lime Cream : 23

CHOPPED CHICKEN LIVERS

Country-Style Coarsely Chopped Chicken Livers with Hard-Cooked Egg, Onion, and a Dash of Brandy : 25

EGGPLANT ANTIPASTO

Diced Eggplant Combined with Onion, Celery, Green Pepper, Tomato, Black Olives, and Capers in a Zesty Tomato Sauce : 26

SKILLET-STEAMED CLAMS

Your choice of Cherrystone or Littleneck Clams Steamed in White Wine and Fresh Garlic, Onion, and Parsley : 28

Soups

STEAKHOUSE-STYLE BEEF BOUILLON

A Rich and Hearty Home-Made Beef Bouillon : 30

CREAM OF CAULIFLOWER SOUP

*A Light and Creamy Soup with Chopped Flowerets of Fresh
Cauliflower and Minced Chives : 31*

JELLIED BEEF BOUILLON

Chilled Jellied Beef Bouillon Laced with Brandy : 32

The Beef

FILET MIGNON WITH BÉARNAISE SAUCE

*A Two-Inch Thick Filet Mignon Topped with Creamy Béarnaise
Sauce : 44*

CRACKED-PEPPER CLUB STEAK

*A Tender and Juicy Steak with a Coating of Coarse Cracked Black
Pepper : 46*

BROILED DOUBLE PORTERHOUSE STEAK

*A Hefty Thick Cut of Beef Charred Black on the Outside and Rosy
Rare Inside : 47*

GARLIC-BROILED SHELL STEAK

A Beefy and Tender Steak Broiled with Garlic Butter : 48

BROASTED BONELESS SIRLOIN

*A Thick Slice of Boneless Sirloin Steak Broiled First and Then Roasted
in the Oven Medium-Rare : 49*

PAN-BROILED RIB EYE STEAK WITH MAÎTRE D'HÔTEL BUTTER

A Small and Juicy Rib Eye Steak Quickly Pan-Broiled and Spread with Parsley-Lemon Butter : 50

ROAST TENDERLOIN OF BEEF

A Thick Cut of Beef Tenderloin Roasted Rare and Served with Broiled Mushroom Caps, Baked Tomato Half, and Deviled Whole Green Beans : 51

SAVORY SLICED SIRLOIN STEAK

Chilled and Marinated Slices of Rare Sirloin Steak Served on a Bed of Spinach Salad : 53

STANDING ROAST RIB OF BEEF

A Thick Slab of Rare or Medium-Rare Roast Beef Served with a Rib : 54

CHOPPED SIRLOIN STEAK

A Full Half Pound of Freshly Ground Sirloin Steak Broiled to Order : 55

Potatoes

BAKED IDAHO POTATO

A Plump and Perfectly Baked Idaho Potato Served with Lightly Salted or Sweet Cream Butter : 61

BAKED POTATO DIABLE IN A "HALF JACKET"

Crumb-Topped Half Potato Baked with Onion, Mustard, and Worcestershire Sauce : 62

CONFETTI-STUFFED BAKED POTATO

Baked Half Potato Stuffed with Onion, Green Pepper, and Pimiento : 63

DOUBLE-CHEESE TWICE-BAKED STUFFED POTATO

Cottage Cheese and Chive-Stuffed Baked Potato with Melted Cheddar Cheese Topping : 64

NEW POTATO IN PARSLEY-CHIVE LEMON BUTTER

Boiled New Potato in a Tangy Parsley and Chive Lemon Butter Sauce : 65

OVEN-ROASTED NEW POTATOES IN JACKETS

Tiny New Potatoes Oven-Roasted to Perfection in their Jackets : 66

YORKSHIRE POTATO PUDDING PUFFS

Light and Fluffy Golden Brown Mashed Potato Puffs : 67

STEAKHOUSE HASH BROWNS

Diced and Browned Fried Potatoes with Onion and Parsley : 68

POTATOES O'BRIEN

Sautéed Potato Cubes Dotted with Onion, Green Pepper, and Pimiento : 69

RED JACKET LYONNAISE POTATOES

Small Red Potatoes Cut into Quarters and Fried in their Jackets with Sweet Red Onion Rings : 70

PAN-BROILED COTTAGE POTATOES

Thin Slices of Brown and Crusty Pan-Broiled Potatoes with a Touch o, Garlic : 71

STEAKHOUSE FRENCH FRIES

The Classic Potato Favorite Fried Crisp and Golden Brown : 72

OVEN-FRIED POTATO STICKS

"French Fries" Prepared Crisp and Golden in the Oven : 73

STEAKHOUSE-STYLE POTATO CHIPS

Melt-in-your-Mouth Crispy-Crunchy Potato Chips : 74

HALF SKINNIES

Butter-Crisp Baked Potato Skins with a Choice of Special
Toppings : 75

Vegetables

BROILED MUSHROOM CAPS

Plump and Juicy Mushroom Caps Broiled with Butter : 79

BAKED TOMATO HALF

A Large Half Tomato Baked with Buttered-Crumb Topping : 80

FRENCH-FRIED ONION RINGS

Melt-in-your-Mouth Crunchy Golden Brown Onion Rings : 81

ZUCCHINI CHIPS

Thin Slices of Zucchini Fried Crisp and Golden : 82

SKILLET-FRIED GREEN TOMATOES

Fried Green Tomato Slices with a Crusty Corn Bread Coating : 83

BROILED GREEN PEPPER

Thick and Tender Slices of Broiled Green Pepper : 84

ASPARAGUS WITH HOLLANDAISE SAUCE

Tender Young Asparagus Spears Topped with a Smooth and Creamy
Hollandaise Sauce : 85

BROCCOLI WITH LEMON DRESSING

Steamed Broccoli Dressed with Lemon and a Touch of Garlic : 87

CREAMED SPINACH

Young Garden-Fresh Spinach in a Rich Cream Sauce : 88

DEVILED GREEN BEANS

Whole Tender Young Green Beans Topped with Deviled Butter : 90

BRAISED RADISHES

Sliced Radishes Braised in a Parsley-Cream Sauce : 91

GREEN PEAS WITH MINT

Shelled Fresh Green Peas with Chopped Fresh Mint : 92

STEAMED BRUSSELS SPROUTS

"Little Cabbages" Steamed and Seasoned with Lemon and Butter : 93

The Salad Bowl

SLICED TOMATOES AND ONIONS

Thick Slices of Beefsteak Tomatoes and Red Onions with Vinaigrette Dressing : 98

SPINACH SALAD

Tender Young Spinach Leaves Tossed with Tomato, Onion, and Celery in a Tart French Dressing and Garnished with Hard-Cooked Egg : 99

CUCUMBERS AND ONIONS IN SOUR CREAM

Paper-Thin Slices of Cucumber and Onion in a Light Sour Cream Dressing : 100

SUPER BOWL

Lettuce, Radishes, Carrot, Celery, Onion, Green Pepper, Tomato, Black Olives, and Parsley, Tossed with a Five-Herb Walnut Vinegar Dressing : 101

CAESAR SALAD

The Classic Romaine Lettuce Salad Tossed with Croutons, Anchovy Fillets, and Parmesan Cheese, in a Distinctive Oil and Vinegar Dressing : 102

BELGIAN ENDIVE WITH ROQUEFORT CREAM DRESSING

Creamy White Endive Topped with a Rich Roquefort Cream Dressing : 103

WHITE CABBAGE COLESLAW

Finely Shredded Crisp White Cabbage Tossed with a Creamy Home-Made Mayonnaise Dressing : 104

RED CABBAGE COLESLAW

Shredded Crisp Red Cabbage, Carrot, and Red Onion, Tossed with a Tart Lemony-Vinegar Dressing : 105

PIMIENTOS, ANCHOVIES, AND CAPERS ON CHOPPED LETTUCE

Pimientos, Anchovies, and Capers on a Bed of Chopped Lettuce with Vinaigrette Dressing : 106

THREE-GREENS SALAD WITH THOUSAND ISLAND DRESSING

Arugula, Radicchio, and Bibb Lettuce, Topped with a Chunky Rich Thousand Island Dressing : 107

DIETERS' SPECIAL SALAD BOWL WITH SIX-CALORIE DRESSING

Your Choice of Escarole, Boston Lettuce, Chicory, or All Three with Special Six-Calorie Tomato Dressing : 108

The Bread Basket

ONION BISCUITS
Flaky Dinner Biscuits Flecked with Onion : 117

TOASTED GARLIC BREAD
Fresh Garlic Baked into Buttery French Bread : 117

GOLDEN CORN BREAD
Rich and Crumbly Golden Corn Bread Squares : 118

SAVORY CRISP RIBBONS
Savory Crisp Seeded Ribbons Baked a Golden Brown : 119

POPOVERS
Light and Puffy Popovers Hot from the Oven : 120

CHEDDAR SQUARES
Baked Golden Brown Bread Squares with Melted Cheddar Cheese : 121

HOME-MADE SODA CRACKERS
Crispy Old-Fashioned Home-Made Soda Crackers : 122

CROUTONS : 123

HOME-MADE SWEET CREAM BUTTER : 125

SEASONED BUTTERS : 126
> *Lightly Salted*
> *Parsley*
> *Chive*
> *Herb*
> *Dill*
> *Onion*
> *Garlic*
> *Lemon*
> *Deviled*

Desserts

OLD-FASHIONED BAKED CUSTARD CUP

A Rich Egg Custard Baked with a Hint of Vanilla : 131

COFFEE RUM ICE CREAM

Home-Made Strong Black Coffee Ice Cream Laced with Rum : 132

FROZEN VANILLA MERINGUE CUSTARD

Luscious Meringue-Filled Frozen Vanilla Custard : 133

BUTTER PECAN ICE CREAM

Roasted Buttery Pecans in a Rich Home-Made Vanilla Ice Cream : 133

HOT CHOCOLATE FUDGE SAUCE

Thick and Gooey Old-Fashioned Hot Chocolate Fudge Sauce : 134

*NOTE
   May We Suggest a Topping of Hot Chocolate Fudge Sauce with Your Choice of Ice Cream

TRIPLE-FRUIT SHERBET

Banana, Orange, and Lemon Blended into a Fresh Fruit Sherbet : 135

LEMON CREAM

Chilled and Tartly Sweet Whipped Lemon Cream : 136

CHOCOLATE CHIFFON PIE WITH WHIPPED CREAM

Light and Fluffy Chocolate Chiffon Pie Served with a Generous Dollop of Whipped Cream : 137

CREAM CHEESECAKE WITH CINNAMON-BUTTER-CRUMB CRUST

A Creamy Smooth Cheesecake with a Spicy Butter Crumb Crust : 138

BUTTERSCOTCH NINE O'CLOCKS

Chewy and Nutty Rich Butterscotch Brownie Squares : 140

POOR-BOY BRANDIED PEACH

A Fresh Peach Half Flamed with Brown Sugar and Brandy : 141

ROQUEFORT CHEESE MOUSSE WITH ASSORTED CRACKERS

Roquefort Cheese Blended into a Creamy Mousse and Served with Assorted Home-Made Crackers : 142

AFTER-DINNER PEPPERMINT WAFERS

Refreshing Home-Made After-Dinner Mints : 143

THE RECIPES

APPETIZERS

SINCE the most important part of any steakhouse dinner is the *beef*, a starter for the meal has to be interesting enough to whet an appetite but light enough not to spoil it. Some of these appetizers are deceptively simple, but worth the little extra effort it takes to make the difference between a special introduction to a meal and an ordinary one.

Vegetable Juice Cocktail with fresh tomatoes and nine other vegetables is a pleasant surprise, because it's home-made. You can serve it in chilled frosted stem glasses or piping hot in earthenware mugs.

Home-made beef bouillon (see And Soups, page 29) is another treat, and it simmers itself slowly and unattended into a rich and hearty broth that's worth the wait.

No steakhouse menu would be complete without a jumbo shrimp cocktail or melon. Only the firmest of real *jumbo*, not merely large, shrimp should be used for the cocktail, and the accompanying recipe for cocktail sauce is just hot enough to awaken but not assault the palate.

Many steakhouses serve raw clams on the half shell, but in the recipe we've included here the clams are gently steamed in their shells with white wine, garlic, onion, and parsley. We saw them served in individual small skillets, which is a nice touch even if your skillets don't match.

If you're preparing your steakhouse dinner for people with healthy appetites, you may want to serve both appetizer *and* soup, but just be sure that everyone leaves enough room to enjoy their beef and the other dishes you've selected from the menu.

Let us begin.

VEGETABLE JUICE COCKTAIL

JUMBO SHRIMP WITH COCKTAIL SAUCE

AVOCADO CUP WITH "HOUSE" FRENCH DRESSING

BROILED MELON SLICES

TOMATO ASPIC WITH WHIPPED LIME CREAM

CHOPPED CHICKEN LIVERS

EGGPLANT ANTIPASTO

SKILLET-STEAMED CLAMS

Vegetable Juice Cocktail

INGREDIENTS

12 medium-size *ripe* tomatoes

1 large stalk celery with leaves, coarsely chopped

2–3 sprigs fresh parsley

3–4 sprigs watercress

3–4 large spinach leaves

1 small onion, coarsely chopped

½ small green pepper, coarsely chopped

1 small carrot, coarsely chopped

1 small white turnip, coarsely chopped

½ small beet, coarsely chopped

½ cup cold water

Salt

¼ teaspoon sugar (optional)

2 tablespoons fresh lemon juice (optional)

PREPARATION

Throughly wash all vegetables. Scrub carrot, white turnip, and beet with a vegetable brush.

Peel onion and remove seeds from green pepper.

Place all vegetables in a large heavy saucepan and add ½ cup cold water.

Simmer vegetables for 1 hour.

Strain vegetable juice into a medium bowl and cover with foil.

Chill.

SERVING

Season vegetable juice to taste before serving in chilled glasses.

Sugar and/or lemon juice may be added.

Note: Vegetable juice may also be served piping hot in mugs.

Jumbo Shrimp with Cocktail Sauce

INGREDIENTS

16 raw dry and firm *jumbo*
   gray-green shrimp in shells
2 quarts water

2 teaspoons salt
Cocktail sauce (see below)

PREPARATION

Wash shrimp under cold running water.

COOKING

Bring water and salt to a boil in a large heavy saucepan.

Drop shrimp into boiling water; shrimp should be completely covered.

When water starts to boil again, reduce heat.

Simmer for 3 to 5 minutes until shrimp turn pink and begin to curl. Do not overcook.

Drain shrimp *immediately*, and rinse under cold running water.

Slit shrimp down the back with a sharp knife and peel off shell.

Pick out the black vein in shrimp carefully with the sharp tip of the knife.

Put shrimp on a plate and cover with foil.

Chill.

COCKTAIL SAUCE

INGREDIENTS

1 cup chili sauce
1 tablespoon fresh lemon juice
1 teaspoon Worcestershire
  sauce
1 teaspoon prepared hot
  horseradish sauce

1 tablespoon celery, minced
  (optional)
1 large lemon, cut into quarters
4 sprigs fresh parsley

PREPARATION

Thoroughly mix all ingredients except lemon wedges and parsley sprigs.

Chill.

Taste sauce before serving, and adjust ingredients to taste.

SERVING

Place a small cup or glass of cocktail sauce in the center of a shallow soup bowl for each serving.

Surround cup or glass with crushed ice.

Arrange four shrimp on ice.

Garnish each serving with a lemon quarter and a sprig of fresh parsley.

Note: Shrimp may be sliced in half before arranging on ice.

Avocado Cup with "House" French Dressing

INGREDIENTS

1 large, ripe avocado

½ cup "House" French Dressing Number Five (see page 110)

4 Bibb or Boston lettuce leaves

1 small pimiento, cut into 4 thin strips

PREPARATION

Chill avocado. *Just before serving*, cut in half and remove stone.

Scoop out pulp carefully with a large spoon, cut into cubes, and place in a small bowl.

Pour French dressing over avocado cubes and mix lightly but well.

Rinse lettuce leaves under cold running water and pat dry with paper towel.

SERVING

Arrange lettuce leaves in the bottom of champagne or favorite stem glasses.

Spoon avocado and dressing into each glass, top with a pimiento strip, and serve immediately.

Broiled Melon Slices

INGREDIENTS

1 ripe medium cantaloupe (or another melon of your choice) sliced 1–1¼ inch thick

2 tablespoons brown sugar

1 tablespoon fresh lemon juice

1 tablespoon fresh lime juice

PREPARATION

Preheat broiler.

Cut cantaloupe crosswise into four rings each 1–1¼ inch thick, remove seeds, and trim off skin.

Sprinkle brown sugar over cantaloupe slices.

Drizzle lemon and lime juices over sugar.

Place cantaloupe slices on a cookie sheet or foil-covered broiler.

Broil 5 minutes, or until golden brown.

SERVING

Serve immediately on small attractive plates.

Note: A dollop of cottage cheese or fresh fruit of your choice may be served in the center of the cantaloupe ring.

Tomato Aspic with Whipped Lime Cream

INGREDIENTS

1 tablespoon unflavored gelatin

2 cups vegetable juice (see Vegetable Juice Cocktail page 19)

1 tablespoon fresh lemon juice

1 teaspoon sugar

Salt

½ small onion, minced

½ small stalk celery, minced (trim off leaves)

4 Bibb or Boston lettuce leaves

Whipped lime cream (see below)

PREPARATION

Chill four salad plates.

Soften gelatin in ½ cup vegetable juice in a small saucepan.

Cook, stirring, over low heat, until gelatin is dissolved.

Add remaining vegetable juice, lemon juice, sugar, and salt. Mix well.

Pour mixture into four individual 1-cup molds with an interesting shape (fluted, ring, a vegetable shape, etc.)

Refrigerate until mixture begins to thicken.

Mix onion and celery in a small bowl.

Stir onion and celery into molds, dividing evenly.

Chill until firm.

WHIPPED LIME CREAM

INGREDIENTS

⅓ cup heavy cream, whipped

½ cup mayonnaise (see Mayonnaise page 110)

2 tablespoons fresh lime juice

Salt

1 tablespoon fresh minced parsley

PREPARATION

Whip cream in a small bowl until thick enough to form a soft peak.

Fold mayonnaise, lime juice, and salt into cream.

Pour mixture into ice cube tray or other shallow container.

Chill in the freezer until cream begins to get firm.

SERVING

Arrange lettuce on chilled salad plates.

Remove gelatin from refrigerator and let cool water run over molds to loosen.

Unmold gelatin onto lettuce.

Remove lime cream from freezer and mix well.

Top gelatin with a generous dollop of lime cream.

Sprinkle with parsley before serving.

Note: Use leftover lime cream for other salads or with chilled soups.

Chopped Chicken Livers

INGREDIENTS

1 pound chicken livers

½ teaspoon salt

2 eggs

1 medium onion, finely chopped

2 tablespoons (¼ stick) butter

1 tablespoon fresh minced parsley

1 ounce brandy

Salt

Freshly ground black pepper

4 Bibb or Boston lettuce leaves

1 large lemon, cut into thin wedges

PREPARATION

Rinse chicken livers with cool water.

Place in boiling salted water in a small saucepan and reduce heat.

Simmer for approximately 15 minutes, or until centers of livers are no longer pink.

Drain livers, and set aside to cool.

Cover eggs with cold water in a small saucepan and bring water to a boil.

Remove the saucepan from heat and cover with a tight-fitting lid.

Let the eggs stand for at least 1 hour.

Run eggs under cold water.

Remove shell.

Sauté onion in butter until golden.

Set aside to cool.

Chop liver, eggs, and onion into a coarse paste in a medium bowl.

Lightly mix in parsley, brandy, and salt and pepper to taste.

Cover liver mixture and chill for 30 minutes.

SERVING

Arrange lettuce leaves on small individual serving plates.

Spoon liver mixture onto lettuce and serve with two or three soda crackers (see recipe page 122) on the side.

Place lemon wedges on each plate.

Eggplant Antipasto

INGREDIENTS

1 small eggplant cut into ½ inch cubes

1 small onion, coarsely chopped

1 small stalk celery, thinly sliced

3 tablespoons olive oil

1 large clove garlic, minced

3 ounces tomato paste

2 tablespoons water

1 small green pepper, cut into ½-inch strips

2 small tomatoes, cut into quarters

3 tablespoons wine vinegar

1 tablespoon sugar

1 tablespoon capers, drained

Generous sprinkling of freshly ground black pepper

Salt

4–5 pitted black olives, thinly sliced

PREPARATION

Wash eggplant under cold running water.

Trim off ends but do not peel.

Cut eggplant into approximately ½-inch cubes.

Note: For easy dicing, cut eggplant into ½-inch horizontal slices and then into ½-inch vertical slices.

Peel onion and chop coarsely.

Wash celery and trim off leaves.

Cut celery stalk into thin slices.

Cut green pepper into ½-inch strips.

Trim off stem end and remove seeds and fibrous portion of pepper. Wash pepper strips inside and out.

Wash tomatoes and trim off stem ends.

Cut tomatoes into quarters.

COOKING

Heat oil in a medium-size heavy skillet or Dutch oven.

Add eggplant cubes, onion, celery, and garlic.

Sauté for approximately 10 minutes until eggplant and onion are golden.

Add tomato paste and water, stir well, and bring just to a boil.

Cover and simmer for 15 minutes.

Add green pepper, tomatoes, and all other ingredients (except olives) to eggplant mixture.

Mix well and cover.

Simmer for 15 minutes.

Remove eggplant mixture from heat and set aside to cool.

Stir in sliced olives when mixture is cool.

Cover eggplant and refrigerate for at least 8 hours.

Mix lightly but well before serving.

SERVING

Serve chilled eggplant on attractive small plates.

Skillet-Steamed Clams

INGREDIENTS

24 cherrystone or littleneck
  raw clams in the shell
1 cup dry white wine
3 tablespoons fresh minced
  parsley

2–3 large cloves garlic, minced
1 medium onion, minced
Salt

PREPARATION

Scrub clams with a stiff brush under cold running water.

Rinse several times, and discard any clam with a gaping or broken shell.

Place clams in a large heavy skillet with a tight-fitting lid.

Add parsley, garlic, and onion. Pour wine over all.

Cover.

Steam clams over medium heat 5 to 7 minutes, or until shells open.

Discard any clam that does not open.

Remove from heat immediately.

Arrange six clams for each serving in small warmed skillets or shallow soup bowls.

Spoon cooking liquid over the clams before serving piping hot.

Salt to taste at the table.

STEAKHOUSE-STYLE BEEF BOUILLON
CREAM OF CAULIFLOWER SOUP
JELLIED BEEF BOUILLON

Steakhouse-Style Beef Bouillon

INGREDIENTS

4–5 pounds meaty shin of beef and marrowbone, cracked and cut up

2 tablespoons marrow (taken from bone)

3 quarts cold water

10 whole black peppercorns

4 cloves

2 bay leaves

4 sprigs fresh parsley

¼ teaspoon dried thyme leaves

¼ teaspoon dried marjoram

1 tablespoon salt

1 large stalk celery, coarsely chopped

1 medium carrot, coarsely chopped

1 small white turnip, coarsely chopped

1 large onion, coarsely chopped

PREPARATION

Have your butcher crack the beef bones, and cut in pieces.

Cut lean meat from bones into small pieces.

Brown ⅓ of meat in the marrow in a small heavy skillet.

Set meat aside to cool.

Put bones and remaining meat in a large heavy kettle.

Cover with 3 quarts of cold water, and let stand for 1 hour.

Add browned meat and all seasonings to kettle.

Bring water to a boil.

Reduce heat and simmer for 5 hours.

Add celery, carrot, turnip, and onion to the kettle.

Simmer for 2 hours.

Rinse several layers of cheesecloth in cold water.

Strain beef stock through these layers of cheesecloth into a large bowl.

Set bowl in a pan of ice water to cool beef stock quickly.

When cool, remove layer of fat which has formed on the top.

SERVING

Reheat 4 cups of beef bouillon until piping hot.

Serve immediately in attractive cups, mugs, or bowls.

Note: Refrigerate extra beef stock, tightly covered, for making other soups and servings.

Cream of Cauliflower Soup

INGREDIENTS

1 small solid white head cauliflower, with unblemished creamy white "curds."

1 cup boiling water

1 cup beef bouillon (see recipe page 30)

2 tablespoons (¼ stick) butter

3 tablespoons flour

1 cup cold water

1 cup half and half

Salt

1 tablespoon fresh minced chives

PREPARATION

Wash cauliflower well under cold running water.

Trim off stem, outer leaves, and the core.

COOKING

Separate flowerets and drop into boiling water in a medium-size heavy saucepan.

Boil uncovered for 5 to 6 minutes.

Remove saucepan from heat, reserve cooking water, and finely chop flowerets.

Do not mash.

Add beef bouillon to cauliflower and its cooking water.

Continue cooking over low heat.

Melt butter in a small saucepan.

Blend in flour and mix thoroughly until smooth.

Add cold water gradually to butter and flour.

Stir until mixture thickens.

Add cream slowly and blend well.

Stir cream mixture into cauliflower and bouillon.

Salt to taste.

Heat soup to just boiling.

Blend well before serving.

SERVING

Serve immediately, piping hot, in small attractive soup bowls.

Sprinkle with chives.

Jellied Beef Bouillon

INGREDIENTS

1 tablespoon unflavored gelatin

¼ cup cold water

2 cups beef bouillon (see recipe page 30)

2 tablespoons sherry

1 tablespoon fresh minced parsley

1 small lemon, cut into quarters

Sour cream (optional)

PREPARATION

Chill four attractive glass goblets.

Soften gelatin in cold water.

Let gelatin soak for 3 minutes in cold water. Do not stir.

Heat beef bouillon just to boiling in a small saucepan.

Remove from heat and add gelatin and sherry.

Stir until smooth and gelatin is dissolved.

Pour mixture into a shallow dish or bowl.

Chill for 4 hours, or until firm.

An hour before serving chill four glass goblets.

SERVING

Spoon jellied bouillon into goblets.

Sprinkle with parsley before serving and garnish with a lemon quarter.

Gelatin may be topped with a dollop of sour cream.

ALL ABOUT BEEF

THE HISTORY OF BEEF in America probably began in the eleventh century when the Vikings brought cattle to Vinland, or Vineland, the name that was given to the northeastern region of North America where the Scandinavians settled. It's interesting to note that *steik* was the old Norse word for meat that the Vikings roasted on spits.

Christopher Columbus is generally credited with bringing the first beef to the Western Hemisphere on his second voyage, but that was just the beginning. Within the next fifty years Juan Ponce de León, who made his fortune as a governor of Puerto Rico and not with the "fountain of youth," had introduced cattle to what is now Florida, and the explorer Francisco Vásquez de Coronado had brought beef into the southwest from Mexico.

When the early settlers began to immigrate from Europe they also increased the cattle population by bringing not only themselves and their few possessions, but the family livestock as well.

We've come a long way since those early days of cattle drives that often stretched out for a mile across the plains, with thousands of head of cattle on the move. While most of the world sleeps, beef comes to market today in streamlined refrigerated trains and trailer trucks. Wholesale meat markets bustle with activity in the early hours of every morning as restaurant men and butchers carefully examine, select, and buy the beef that eventually comes to your table.

This is finicky shopping at its most demanding! The buyers go over a check list of things to look for, including conformation and age of the beef; weight; color; texture; marbling; fat; smell; to name a few points that determine quality. Fortunately the quality of cattle has been constantly improved by selective and scientific breeding, with the result that now we are able to enjoy some of the world's finest beef.

We won't concern ourselves here with the names of the many breeds of cattle, since it's more important for you to know about the beef you'll be buying and those cuts that make the difference between a merely *good* steak and a *superb* one. The first important step in buying beef—or any meat for that matter—is finding a butcher you can trust and one with whom you have complete rapport. You should be able to rely on him to let you know about any beef specials that are going to be on sale; to cut and trim your purchases to order; and since butchers are usually good cooks, he may even share a recipe or two with you.

If you already have such a butcher we don't have to tell you how lucky you are. Whether he works in a market or in a specialty shop that sells only meat, your butcher is the man who will be ultimately responsible for the success of your "steakhouse" dinner.

You may have difficulty buying *prime* beef, since it's sold almost exclusively to hotels and restaurants. A quality and expensive meat market may carry or order it for you, but don't expect to find prime-graded beef in many supermarkets. It's simply too expensive and too scarce.

And expensive it will be, but worth every cent you'll have to spend!

Prime is the top grade of beef sold in the United States. It is so expensive because only one out of every three or four steers becomes prime beef. Also, the consumer must eventually absorb the cost of aging the meat. Sides of beef are hung in a climate-controlled cold box or cooler at temperatures of 34°–38° until they "ripen," which means that natural enzymes are activated during the aging process to break down tissue and make the beef more tender. As much as fifteen percent of the weight of the beef is lost as the natural moisture in the meat evaporates, and a dry exterior covering develops that must be trimmed off. Even the finest cuts of prime beef will lack tenderness and a rich beefy flavor if they're not aged for at least two weeks. The longer beef hangs, the "beefier" tasting it becomes, and steakhouses and butchers who carry prime age their beef from two to four weeks, and sometimes longer. Only *prime* and some heavy cuts of *choice* beef are aged. The United States Department of Agriculture grades beef sold by the wholesale packing companies on the basis of nationally uniform federal standards of quality. There are several consumer grades of beef on the market but in this book we will discuss only *prime* and *choice*, (an excellent grade of beef that you probably buy most often in your market). Choice beef has less exterior fat covering than prime and very little marbling.

Your butcher can be helpful, but you should have some knowledge of your own about what to look for when buying a steak. This is a basic ten-point guide from the experts:

1. *Look for prime* beef, and *choice* second if *prime* is not available. Try specialty butcher shops, and some wholesalers occasionally sell prime beef retail if your bill totals a specified amount. Mail order *prime* steaks are a possibility (see page 57). As a last resort, a steakhouse where you're a regular customer might sell you *prime* steaks for a special occasion (but don't make a habit of asking!).

2. *Look for* a delicately woven marbling of creamy white fat running through the steak.

3. *Look for* steak that has an outside layer of firm and creamy white fat that flakes when you scratch it with your fingernail.

4. *Look for* a light and clean fresh smell from the beef.

5. *Avoid* thick marbling through the steak, which means tough beef.

6. *Avoid* beef that has no marbling, even though the meat may look lean and tender.

7. *Avoid* a dark red color; beef should be a healthy cherry red.

8. *Avoid* any steak that is two-tone red with light and dark sections in the beef.

9. *Avoid* beef that has excessive moisture.

10. *Avoid* beef that has a coarse rather than a smooth and silky blood texture.

The four different cuts of beef that steakhouses use have distinctly different textures and tastes, so you'll want to experiment until you find which cut you prefer. It's not enough to ask your butcher for "a thick steak" or "four small steaks" when it's so easy to familiarize yourself with the names of specific cuts. Many people like a boneless steak, while others don't feel as though they're eating a steak at all if the familiar T-bone or rib has been boned out. Whatever your preference, your butcher will appreciate your being able to order the steak by its name.

We've discussed what to look for when buying beef, now these are the cuts for the steaks:

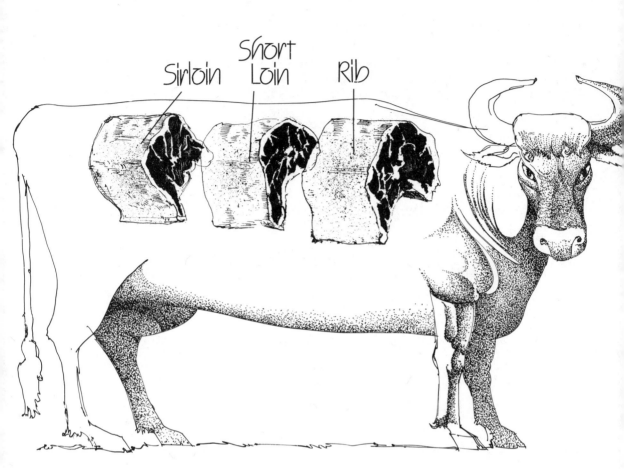

RIB

Standing Rib Roast
Rib Steak

and

Rib Eye Steak
Delmonico Steak
Spencer Steak

A standing rib roast for roast beef is cut from this section close to the loin, which will give you an idea of the taste and texture of a *rib steak*. A rib steak is a thick, meaty, tender piece of beef attached to one rib bone. When a rib steak is trimmed and boned down to the "heart" it becomes a boneless *rib eye, Delmonico,* or *Spencer steak.*

For Economy: Buy a three-rib standing roast and have your butcher cut it into rib steaks or boneless *rib eye steaks* that will leave an assortment of bones and meat left over for other uses; or trim the roast yourself.

Buy a whole beef *rib eye roast* and have your butcher cut it into *rib eye steaks*; or cut the steaks yourself.

LOIN (or Short Loin)

T-Bone Steak
Porterhouse Steak
Shell Steak
Top Loin Steak

and

Tenderloin Steak
Filet Mignon
Strip Steak

T-bone and *porterhouse* are big, impressive, fine-textured, and tender steaks that taste as beefy and good as they look. The porterhouse has a bigger tenderloin than the T-bone steak, and is particularly popular because with a few cuts from a butcher's knife (or your own) you can have both a *shell steak* plus a *filet mignon* at *porterhouse* prices. Be sure these steaks are trimmed well, since you'll pay a premium if the heavy and relatively tough tail is left on.

For Economy: If you find a good buy on a *porterhouse steak* with the tail left on, ask your butcher to grind the tail for a hamburger patty. The patty can be broiled and served in place of the tail when the steak is served.

SIRLOIN

Pin Bone Sirloin Steak
Flat Bone Sirloin Steak
Round Bone Sirloin Steak
Wedge Bone Sirloin Steak

and

Boneless Sirloin Steak

Sirloin is less expensive than a *rib* or *short loin steak*, and it has a good beefy flavor and a nice texture. Sirloin steaks vary in size and shape, and they're a popular cut with or without the bone that gives them their name. The *pin bone* and *flat bone* are tender sirloins closest to the short loin and they have large filets.

For Economy: Buy a thick *sirloin steak* with a large tenderloin, and have your butcher cut it into *boneless steaks* and *filet mignons*; or do it yourself. You'll have extra beef left over for hamburger and kabobs.

TENDERLOIN OF BEEF

Filet Mignon
Chateaubriand
Tournedo
Filet Steak

The *beef tenderloin* is the most tender and expensive of all the beef cuts. The *tenderloin* is a long, slender piece of beef that rests inside the full *loin*. There are only two *tenderloins* to each steer and they are relatively small, which partly accounts for their high cost. This is beef of the highest order if you want melt-in-your-mouth tenderness and not a heavy beef flavor. When sliced the *tenderloin of beef* becomes silky, boneless *filet mignons, Châteaubriand, tournedos,* and *filet steaks*.

For Economy: Look for a sale and buy a whole *tenderloin of beef*, which may weigh up to only 6 pounds. Have your butcher slice it into all of the above, and a small roast from the thick end; or do it yourself. You'll have a bit of beef left over for kabobs, or the world's most expensive hamburger.

If you're going to try your hand at doing your own meat-cutting, you'll want to invest in one of the excellent how-to books on the market that offer step-by-step instruction. It's not easy in the beginning and it takes patience, but if you want to enjoy steak more often you can save money by cutting and trimming cuts of beef yourself. You'll also need good quality knives for cutting and boning the steaks, and these knives should be kept sharpened and in good condition at all times; even when they're not in use.

A meat grinder is necessary and a great money-saver if you serve hamburger often. You can take advantage of leftovers from the various cuts of beef you buy, and grind them into deluxe chopped steak just like the restaurants serve. You can also buy beef for grinding when there are special sales. We like the old-fashioned manual meat grinder, but there are many electric models available that are undoubtedly easier to use, and you can buy an attachment for your blender that grinds meat, or use a food processor fitted with a metal blade.

ALL ABOUT COOKING BEEF

There's an old axiom that if you want to see a steakhouse man cry, you have only to order your beef "well done," or even "medium well." The consensus among restaurateurs and chefs is that rare or medium-rare is the only way top quality beef should be cooked, and anything more is a sacrilege. Heat does solidify protein, and beef cooked past medium-rare will naturally be less tender than the steak cooked for a shorter time.

A hot broiler is a big plus in cooking steaks to perfection, and since professional steakhouse broilers fire up to temperatures as high as 1400° Fahrenheit it's little wonder that your steak comes to the table beautifully charred black on the outside and rosy rare on the inside. Steakhouse "broiler men" have an uncanny sixth sense that lets them know just when a steak is done, *exactly* as ordered. Theirs is an art that comes from practice and experience but also, surprisingly, touch. The longer a steak cooks, the firmer it becomes. You can test if a steak is done rare or medium-rare by the amount of "give" it has when you press the meat quickly with your fingers. If it depresses easily, you could be well on your way to serving a perfectly cooked steak, but don't be discouraged if the touch test doesn't work the first few times you try it. You may need to develop more of that sixth sense that enables top "broiler men" to watch over a dozen or more steaks at a time.

In restaurant language all steaks are broiled rare, medium-rare, and with some concession medium, and charred to crusty black perfection on the outside. Rare is red all the way through with a tepid center; medium-rare is rosy red all the way through with a warmer center; medium is a bright pink all the way through. And then there's black and blue—black on the outside and blue on the inside—for those who mean it when they order their steak *"rare."*

Even though your broiler at home can't approximate the super high temperatures of the professional stoves, you can still do a creditable job of turning out a superb steak. These are a few tips from the steakhouses that will help:

1. Preheat your broiler at highest temperature for 30 minutes.

2. Remove steak from refrigerator at least 1 hour before cooking so that it will be at room temperature.

3. Pat the steak dry just before cooking so that there is no moisture on the meat.

4. Season the beef after, not before, cooking.

5. Rub the outside layer of fat lightly with fresh lemon to prevent scorching or burning.

6. Brush the steak with olive oil (if you're using an oil), which won't burn before the beef cooks.

7. Score the outside layer of fat to keep the steak from curling.

8. A steak should be no less than 1 inch thick, and preferably thicker for broiling.

9. Steak should be broiled on a wire rack or broiler tray over a broiler pan that allows air to circulate under the beef.

10. Steaks 1–1½ inches thick should be broiled 2–3 inches away from the heat.

11. Steaks 2 inches and thicker should be broiled 3–5 inches away from the heat.

12. The steak should be turned as little as possible during broiling, and no more than three times.

13. It's always better to undercook a steak than to overestimate cooking time. If the beef is too rare it can be put back under the broiler for a few minutes, while an overdone steak is a total disaster that can't be remedied.

Note: Always prewarm serving plates in the oven.

FILET MIGNON WITH BÉARNAISE SAUCE
CRACKED-PEPPER CLUB STEAK
BROILED DOUBLE PORTERHOUSE STEAK
GARLIC-BROILED SHELL STEAK
BROASTED BONELESS SIRLOIN
PAN-BROILED RIB EYE STEAK WITH
  MAÎTRE D'HÔTEL BUTTER
ROAST TENDERLOIN OF BEEF
SAVORY SLICED SIRLOIN STEAK
STANDING ROAST RIB OF BEEF
CHOPPED SIRLOIN STEAK

Filet Mignon with Béarnaise Sauce

THE BEEF

Have butcher prepare and trim beef tenderloin for 4 filet mignons 2 inches thick.

INGREDIENTS

1 beef tenderloin
   approximately 8 inches long
Brandy
Freshly ground black pepper

4 strips bacon (optional)
1 tablespoon butter
Béarnaise sauce (see below)

PREPARATION

Preheat broiler.

Sprinkle beef tenderloin with brandy and wrap in a clean white cloth.

Let stand for 30 minutes.

Slice tenderloin into 4 steaks 2 inches thick (if the butcher hasn't prepared).

Sprinkle steaks with freshly ground black pepper.

If using bacon, wrap a strip around edge of each steak and secure with a toothpick.

Dot each steak with a small piece of butter.

COOKING

Place steaks on a broiler rack or tray 4 inches away from heat.

Broil for 3 to 5 minutes.

Turn steaks and broil for 3 to 5 minutes on other side.

BÉARNAISE SAUCE

INGREDIENTS

2 egg yolks

2 tablespoons light cream

3 tablespoons dry white wine

1 tablespoon tarragon vinegar

1 bay leaf

4 whole peppercorns

½ teaspoon salt

Pinch cayenne

¾ cup butter, melted

2 tablespoons fresh minced parsley

2 tablespoons fresh finely chopped chives

¼ teaspoon tomato paste

1 teaspoon fresh lemon juice

PREPARATION

Put egg yolks in a small bowl and stir in cream.

Boil wine, vinegar, bay leaf, and peppercorns down to 2 tablespoons in a small saucepan.

Set aside to cool.

When cool, strain mixture into egg yolks and cream.

Add salt and cayenne.

Place bowl over but not in a saucepan of boiling water.

Whisk until mixture begins to thicken.

Add butter, slowly whisking all the while until sauce is thick and creamy.

Throughly blend in parsley, chives, tomato paste, and lemon juice.

SERVING

Remove steaks to individual serving plates.

Spoon Béarnaise sauce over each filet mignon and serve immediately.

Cracked-Pepper Club Steak

THE BEEF

Have butcher prepare and trim 4 club steaks, each approximately 1½ inches thick.

INGREDIENTS

1 tablespoon crushed black peppercorns

4 club steaks, each approximately 1½ inches thick

2 teaspoons salt

PREPARATION

Crush whole black peppercorns with a mallet or rolling pin to make 1 tablespoon of coarse pepper.

Press pepper into both sides of each steak, using the heel of your hand.

Sprinkle salt over the bottom of a large heavy cast-iron skillet.

Heat skillet until salt begins to brown.

Place steaks in skillet and sear over high heat for approximately 3 minutes on each side.

Reduce heat and cook steaks for 2 to 3 minutes on each side.

SERVING

Remove steaks to individual serving plates and serve immediately.

Broiled Double Porterhouse Steak

THE BEEF

Have butcher prepare and trim 2 porterhouse steaks, each 2–2½ inches thick.

INGREDIENTS

1 tablespoon olive oil	Lemon wedge
2 large cloves garlic, crushed	Salt
2 porterhouse steaks, each 2–2½ inches thick	Freshly ground black pepper

PREPARATION

Combine oil and garlic and spread over steaks on both sides. Let stand for 1 hour.

Score outside layer of fat on both steaks and rub with lemon.

COOKING

Preheat broiler for 30 minutes.

Place steaks on broiler rack or tray 4 inches away from heat.

Broil for 9 to 10 minutes, turn steaks and broil 9 to 10 minutes on other side.

Remove steaks to carving board.

SERVING

Season steaks with salt and pepper.

Slice and serve immediately on individual platters.

Note: Steaks may be served with Broiled Mushroom Caps (see recipe page 79)

Garlic-Broiled Shell Steak

THE BEEF

Have butcher prepare and trim 4 shell steaks, each approximately 1½ inches thick.

INGREDIENTS

4 tablespoons (½ stick) butter
3–4 large cloves garlic, crushed
4 shell steaks, each approximately 1½ inches thick

PREPARATION

Preheat broiler.

Melt butter with crushed garlic in a small saucepan.

Brush steaks on one side with garlic butter.

COOKING

Place steaks on broiler rack or tray 3 inches away from heat.

Broil for 6 to 7 minutes.

Turn steaks and brush with garlic butter.

Broil for 5 to 6 minutes.

SERVING

Remove steaks to individual serving plates.

Serve immediately.

THE BEEF

Have butcher prepare and trim 3–3½ pounds of boneless sirloin steak, 2 inches thick.

INGREDIENTS

**3–3½ pounds boneless sirloin
  steak, 2 inches thick**
1 tablespoon olive oil
1 tablespoon butter, softened
Salt
Freshly ground black pepper

PREPARATION

Preheat broiler.

Pat steak dry with paper towel.

Rub both sides of steak with oil.

Place steak on a rack in a shallow flameproof dish.

COOKING

Place steak under broiler 4 inches from heat.

Broil 2 to 3 minutes.

Turn steak and broil 2 to 3 minutes on other side.

Remove steak from broiler.

Reduce heat to 375°.

Spread softened butter over steak on each side.

Place steak in top third of oven.

Roast for 10 to 12 minutes.

Remove steak from oven to a carving board.

Season with salt and pepper.

Cut steak on the diagonal into thick slices.

SERVING

Place slices on individual serving plates and serve immediately.

Pan-Broiled Rib Eye Steak With
Maître D'Hôtel Butter

THE BEEF

Have butcher prepare and trim 4 rib eye steaks each 1 inch thick.

INGREDIENTS

4 rib eye steaks, each 1 inch thick
Salt
Freshly ground black pepper
Maître d'Hôtel Butter (see below)

PREPARATION

Slowly heat a large heavy cast-iron skillet. Test temperature with a small piece of fat cut from steak that will sizzle when it touches the pan.

Rub pan lightly with the same piece of fat if steaks are very lean.

Place steaks in skillet and let them sizzle nicely until seared brown, 4 to 5 minutes.

Turn steaks and brown 4 to 5 minutes on other side.

Pour off any fat from skillet as it accumulates during cooking.

Season with salt and pepper.

MAÎTRE D'HÔTEL BUTTER

INGREDIENTS

¼ cup butter, softened

2 teaspoons fresh finely
  chopped parsley

1 tablespoon fresh lemon juice

½ teaspoon salt, or to taste

⅛ teaspoon white pepper

PREPARATION

Cream butter in a small bowl until smooth.

Blend in parsley, lemon juice, salt, and pepper.

SERVING

Remove steaks from skillet to individual serving plates.

Spread hot steaks with Maître d'Hôtel Butter and serve immediately.

Note: All other steaks 1 inch thick may be pan-broiled as with rib eye steak. The steaks should be no thicker than 1 inch. Maître d'Hôtel Butter optional.

Roast Tenderloin of Beef

THE BEEF

Have butcher prepare a beef tenderloin for four.

INGREDIENTS

1 beef tenderloin for four that
  will be cut into steaks 2½–3
  inches thick after cooking.

Olive oil, for pan

4 tablespoons (½ stick) butter,
  softened

Salt

Freshly ground black pepper

PREPARATION

Preheat oven to 500°.

Place beef on a rack in an oiled shallow roasting pan.

Coat the beef thoroughly with butter.

Place in oven, and reduce heat immediately to 400°.

COOKING

Roast for 25 to 30 minutes.

Do not turn, baste, or cover the tenderloin.

If you use a meat thermometer, the internal temperature of the beef should be 130° for rare.

Remove beef from oven to carving board.

Season with salt and freshly ground black pepper.

Slice tenderloin into 4 servings 2½–3 inches thick

SERVING

Arrange slices of beef on a large silver or other elegant serving platter.

Surround with Broiled Mushroom Caps, Baked Tomato Halves, and whole Deviled Green Beans (see recipes pages 78).

Savory Sliced Sirloin Steak

THE BEEF

Have butcher prepare and trim 2 pounds of boneless sirloin steak, 2 inches thick.

INGREDIENTS

2 pounds boneless sirloin steak 2 inches thick

1 tablespoon olive oil

Spinach Salad (see Spinach Salad page 99)

MARINADE

1⅓ cups olive oil

1 cup white wine vinegar

2 scallions, finely chopped

1 small stalk celery, finely chopped

2 large cloves garlic, minced

1 tablespoon Dijon mustard

1 teaspoon Worcestershire sauce

1 tablespoon prepared hot horseradish

1 teaspoon salt

Freshly ground black pepper

PREPARATION

Preheat broiler.

Pat steak dry with paper towel.

Rub both sides of steak with 1 tablespoon oil.

Place steak on broiler rack or tray 4 inches away from heat.

Broil for 8 to 9 minutes.

Turn steak and broil for 8 to 9 minutes on other side.

Remove steak from broiler and set aside to cool.

Combine 1⅓ cups oil and the vinegar with all other ingredients except spinach in a glass jar with a tight-fitting lid. Shake well.

Cut steak into slices ¼–½ inch thick.

Arrange slices in a single layer on a large platter or dish.

Pour oil and vinegar mixture over steak.

Cover with plastic and refrigerate for 8 hours.

Baste steak occasionally with marinade.

Remove steak from marinade.

SERVING

Arrange a bed of spinach salad on four serving plates.

Place slices of steak on top of spinach.

Serve.

Standing Roast Rib of Beef

THE BEEF

Have butcher prepare and trim a 2-rib standing beef roast.

INGREDIENTS

1 2-rib standing beef roast
Olive oil, for pan
Salt
Freshly ground black pepper

PREPARATION

Remove beef from refrigerator 2 hours before roasting.

Preheat oven to 500°.

Place standing roast fat side up in a lightly oiled shallow roasting pan. The roast should rest on the end of its ribs to lift it off the pan. No rack is necessary.

Sprinkle roast with salt and pepper.

Insert a meat thermometer into center of roast. To determine exact center, line the thermometer up against the cut side of beef with the point at the center where the thermometer will rest. The thermometer should not touch fat or bone.

COOKING

Roast for 15 minutes and reduce heat to 350°.

Roast beef for 18 to 20 minutes per pound for rosy rare, or until the internal temperature of the beef is 140° on the thermometer.

Do not cover beef or add water during roasting.

SERVING

Remove roast beef from oven to carving board at the table.

Place roast on its side.

Carve slices 1½ inches thick, with or without a rib.

Serve slices on individual small platters.

Chopped Sirloin Steak

THE BEEF

Have butcher grind 2 pounds of boneless sirloin steak, or grind the beef yourself just before using.

INGREDIENTS

2 pounds ground boneless sirloin steak shaped into 4 patties 2-inches thick

2 tablespoons (¼ stick) butter, softened

Salt

Freshly ground black pepper

PREPARATION

Preheat broiler.

Shape ground beef lightly into 4 patties 2 inches thick, handle the beef as little as possible.

COOKING

Place patties on a broiler rack or tray 4 inches away from heat.

Dot patties with half the softened butter.

Broil for 5 minutes.

Turn patties and dot with the rest of the butter.

Broil for 3 to 5 minutes depending on desired loneness.

SERVING

Remove patties to individual serving plates.

Season at the table with salt and pepper to taste.

*ORDER TOP QUALITY PRIME
BEEF BY MAIL FROM:*

STOCK YARDS PACKING COMPANY
340 North Oakley Blvd.
Chicago, Illinois 60612

BALDUCCI'S
424 Avenue of the Americas
Greenwich Village, New York
    10011

POTATOES

NOW THAT you've selected the beef for your meal, we come to the all-important potato—baked, stuffed, fried, boiled, roasted, and served in all its glory!

From its sixteenth century beginnings in South America as an ornamental plant, the potato has had an illustrious history. Odes have been written in praise of it; songs have been sung to it; and of course no steakhouse dinner would be complete without a potato on the plate.

From the fifteen choices included on the menu, you can prepare either a light or more substantial potato recipe depending on what other vegetables and salad you're serving. One of the stuffed baked potatoes always goes nicely with a filet mignon or other small steak. Oven-Fried Potato Sticks, Steakhouse-Style Potato Chips, or Half Skinnies don't crowd a heavyweight porterhouse or big sirloin, and they make an appetizing side dish for a big steak.

Idaho and Maine potatoes are favorites of the steakhouses for baking into mealy perfection, but potatoes from other areas can be used as long as they're *mature* and have good skins. Young potatoes should not be used for baking, and while the potatoes sold in your market year round are all-purpose, they're not recommended for baking. The new potatoes that are harvested in the spring before they're fully mature are a special treat when they're available, and the recipes here coat them in Parsley-Chive Lemon Butter and oven-roast them in their jackets. All the favorite steakhouse-style potatoes are included on the menu, but since the classic Baked Idaho Potato is one of the most famous of all, our recipes begin with this simple but elegant "steakmate."

BAKED IDAHO POTATO

BAKED POTATO DIABLE IN A "HALF JACKET"

CONFETTI-STUFFED BAKED POTATO

DOUBLE-CHEESE TWICE-BAKED STUFFED POTATO

NEW POTATO IN PARSELY-CHIVE LEMON BUTTER

OVEN-ROASTED NEW POTATOES IN JACKETS

YORKSHIRE POTATO PUDDING PUFFS

STEAKHOUSE HASH BROWNS

POTATOES O'BRIEN

RED JACKET LYONNAISE POTATOES

PAN-BROILED COTTAGE POTATOES

STEAKHOUSE FRENCH FRIES

OVEN-FRIED POTATO STICKS

STEAKHOUSE-STYLE POTATO CHIPS

HALF SKINNIES

Baked Idaho Potato

INGREDIENTS

4 Idaho or other baking
  potatoes, nicely shaped and
  of equal size

Corn or peanut oil

8 tablespoons (1 stick) butter,
  divided into four servings

Salt

Freshly ground black pepper
  or white pepper

Sour cream (optional)

PREPARATION

Wash and scrub potatoes with a vegetable brush, and dry
thoroughly.

Rub potatoes generously with corn or peanut oil for a soft skin.
Use less oil if a crisper skin is desired.

COOKING

Preheat oven to 425°.

Place potatoes on oven rack and bake for approximately 45 minutes,
or until potatoes are soft when pressed together with fingers (use
an oven mitt or glove).

SERVING

Remove potatoes from oven and slit across the top.

Press potatoes open with fingers, and push a piece of butter into
each potato.

Serve immediately on individual side dishes. Season individually
at the table with more butter, salt, freshly ground black pepper, or
white pepper. Sour cream served in an attractive white bowl or
serving dish is optional.

Baked Potato Diable in a "Half Jacket"

INGREDIENTS

2 large Idaho or other baking
potatoes of equal size

2 teaspoons prepared yellow
mustard of your choice

1 small onion, minced

2 teaspoons Worcestershire
sauce

Pinch salt

¼ cup fine dry bread crumbs

4 pats butter

PREPARATION

Wash and scrub potatoes with a vegetable brush.

COOKING

Place potatoes in boiling water and cook for 20 to 25 minutes, or
until just tender and nearly cooked through.

Preheat oven to 450°.

Pour off water and dry potatoes *thoroughly*.

Split each potato lengthwise into halves.

Spread each potato half with mustard, and sprinkle with onion,
Worcestershire sauce, and a little salt.

Top with bread crumbs and a pat of butter.

Place potatoes on a cookie sheet or foil.

Bake for 15 to 20 minutes until potatoes are cooked through and
crumbs are nicely browned.

SERVING

Serve immediately on individual side dishes.

Confetti-Stuffed Baked Potato

INGREDIENTS

2 large Idaho or other baking
 potatoes (see Baked Idaho
 Potato page 61)
2 tablespoons (¼ stick) butter
1–2 tablespoons warm heavy
 cream

Salt
1 small onion, minced
½ small green pepper, minced
1 small pimiento, drained and
 finely chopped

PREPARATION

Split each baked potato lengthwise into halves.

Scoop out the inside of the halves, being careful not to break the skins.

Whip potato pulp, butter, and warm heavy cream in a small bowl until fluffy.

Add salt to taste.

Thoroughly mix in onion, green pepper, and pimiento.

Pile potato mixture lightly onto potato skins. Do not pat down the top.

COOKING

Place potato halves on a cookie sheet.

Bake in 425° oven until tops are lightly browned.

SERVING

Serve immediately on the same plate as the beef.

Double-Cheese Twice-Baked Stuffed Potato

INGREDIENTS

4 large Idaho or other baking potatoes (see Baked Idaho Potato page 61)

4 tablespoons (½ stick) butter

1 cup low-fat or regular creamed cottage cheese

2 tablespoons heavy cream

1 tablespoon fresh minced chives

Salt

Sprinkling of white pepper (optional)

½ cup grated Cheddar cheese

Paprika

PREPARATION

Cut a thin slice lengthwise from top of each baked potato.

Raise oven temperature to 450°.

Scoop out the inside of potatoes, being careful not to break the skins.

Throughly mash potato with butter in a medium bowl.

Blend in all other ingredients except Cheddar cheese and paprika.

Pile potato mixture into skins. Do not pat down the top.

Sprinkle potato tops with Cheddar cheese and paprika.

COOKING

Place potatoes on a cookie sheet.

Bake in 450° ove for 10 to 15 minutes, or until potatoes are heated through and cheese melts.

SERVING

Serve immediately on individual side dishes.

New Potato in Parsley-Chive Lemon Butter

INGREDIENTS

4 medium new potatoes,
   nicely shaped and of equal
   size

4 tablespoons (½ stick) butter

1 tablespoon fresh lemon juice

1 heaping teaspoon fresh
   minced parsley

1 heaping teaspoon
   minced fresh chives

Salt

White pepper

PREPARATION

Wash potatoes under cold running water.

COOKING

Place potatoes in gently boiling water and cook for 15 to 20 minutes, or until tender. Drain, and carefully peel off skins.

Melt butter in a medium saucepan.

Stir in lemon juice, parsley, chives, salt to taste, and sprinkling of white pepper.

Add potatoes to butter.

Turn each potato carefully until thoroughly coated with the parsley-chive butter mixture.

Turn up heat for 1 minute.

SERVING

Serve potatoes piping hot on individual side dishes.

Oven-Roasted New Potatoes in Jackets

INGREDIENTS

12 to 16 small, nicely shaped
new potatoes

6 tablespoons (¾ stick) butter,
melted

Freshly ground black pepper

PREPARATION

Wash potatoes under cold running water.

COOKING

Preheat oven to 350°.

Place potatoes in gently boiling water and cook for 5 minutes. Drain.

Arrange potatoes in a shallow baking dish.

Brush generously with 4 tablespoons of melted butter and roast for approximately 15 minutes or until potatoes are tender.

Baste potatoes with the remaining melted butter while they're roasting.

SERVING

Serve three or four potatoes on the same plate with the beef, and sprinkle with freshly ground black pepper.

Yorkshire Potato Pudding Puffs

INGREDIENTS

2 eggs, separated

2 cups warm mashed potatoes
(from the Half Skinnies
page 75)

2 tablespoons hot milk

1 tablespoon fresh parsley,
finely chopped

½ teaspoon onion, minced

Salt

2 tablespoons (¼ stick)
softened butter

PREPARATION

Preheat oven to 350°.

Put yolks in a medium bowl.

Beat egg yolks briskly until they begin to get thick and creamy.

Add mashed potatoes, milk, parsley, onion, and salt to taste.

Whisk potatoes until fluffy.

Beat egg whites until stiff, and fold into potato mixture.

COOKING

Generously butter an 8-cup muffin tin. (Or potato mixture may be placed in mounds on a buttered cookie sheet.)

Spoon mixture into muffin tin and place a softened butter pat on top of each serving.

Bake approximately 20 minutes or until potato puffs are golden brown.

SERVING

Serve immediately on the same plate as the beef or on individual side dishes.

Steakhouse Hash Browns

INGREDIENTS

4 medium all-purpose potatoes, peeled and finely diced

3 tablespoons corn or peanut oil

1 tablespoon fresh minced parsley

1 small onion, finely chopped

½ teaspoon salt

Generous sprinkling freshly ground black pepper

Flour

¼ cup heavy cream

PREPARATION

Wash, peel, and finely dice raw potatoes.

COOKING

Heat oil in a medium-size heavy skillet.

Combine diced potatoes, parsley, onion, salt, and pepper.

Add potatoes to skillet and sprinkle lightly with flour.

Press potatoes down with spatula into a flat cake.

Sauté potatoes, lifting them lightly with the spatula as they begin to brown so they won't stick to the skillet.

When bottom is brown, cut the potato cake in quarters.

Turn each quarter carefully with the spatula.

Pour heavy cream over potatoes.

Brown underside of the potato quarters.

SERVING

Serve immediately piping hot on the same plate as the beef or on individual side dishes.

Potatoes O'Brien

INGREDIENTS

4 medium all-purpose
  potatoes, peeled and cut
  into cubes

3 tablespoons corn or peanut
  oil

Salt

1 small onion, finely chopped

1 small green pepper, finely
  diced

1 medium pimiento, finely
  diced

Freshly ground black pepper

1 tablespoon butter (optional)

PREPARATION

Wash, peel, and cut raw potatoes into approximately ½-inch cubes.

COOKING

Cover potato cubes with cold water in a small saucepan.

Bring water to a boil and simmer potatoes for 2 minutes.

Drain potato cubes and pat dry on paper towel.

Heat oil in a medium-size heavy skillet.

Add potatoes to skillet and sprinkle with salt.

Sauté potatoes, tossing them lightly with a fork, for approximately
8 minutes or until golden.

Add onion and green pepper.

Continue cooking and turning potatoes gently with a fork for approximately 3 minutes. Do not press potato cubes flat into skillet.

Add pimiento and freshly ground black pepper to taste, with 1
tablespoon of butter, (optional).

Cook potato mixture for approximately 2 minutes, and toss lightly.

SERVING

Serve immediately on the same plate as the beef or on individual
side dishes.

Red Jacket Lyonnaise Potatoes

INGREDIENTS

12 small red potatoes with good skins

2 tablespoons corn or peanut oil

1 tablespoon butter

1 small red onion, thinly sliced

2 tablespoons fresh finely chopped parsley

Salt

Freshly ground black pepper

PREPARATION

Wash potatoes under cold running water.

COOKING

Place potatoes in boiling water. Reduce heat and simmer for approximately 20 minutes, or until tender.

Drain potatoes and let cool.

Cut potatoes into quarters with skins.

Heat oil and butter in a medium-size heavy skillet.

Add potatoes to skillet and sauté, turning them carefully with a spatula, for approximately 5 minutes or until golden brown.

Add onion and parsley.

Continue cooking and turning potatoes gently with spatula for approximately 3 minutes, or until onions are soft.

Season with salt and freshly ground black pepper to taste.

SERVING

Serve immediately on individual side dishes.

Pan-Broiled Cottage Potatoes

INGREDIENTS

3 large mature potatoes, with good unblemished skins for frying

2 tablespoons (¼ stick) butter

2 tablespoons corn or peanut oil

1 small onion, finely chopped

2–3 cloves garlic, minced

½ teaspoon salt, or to taste

Freshly ground black pepper to taste

PREPARATION

Wash and scrub potatoes with a vegetable brush.

Thinly slice or finely chop raw potatoes with skins

COOKING

Heat butter and oil with onion and garlic in a large heavy skillet until hot, but not sizzling.

Add potatoes to skillet and press down with spatula into a ¼–½-inch flat cake.

Reduce heat to medium low and cover skillet. Cook approximately 10 minutes, or until brown and crusty.

Turn potatoes carefully with spatula. Brown potatoes on the other side until cooked through and brown and crisp, approximately 10 minutes.

Season with salt and freshly ground black pepper.

SERVING

Serve immediately piping hot on individual side dishes.

Steakhouse French Fries

INGREDIENTS

4 mature baking potatoes, peeled and cut into strips

Corn or peanut oil for deep-frying

Salt

PREPARATION

Wash, peel, and cut raw potatoes into strips ¼–½-inch thick, and approximately 2½ inches long.

Soak potatoes in ice water for 1 hour.

Drain potatoes and pat *throughly* dry on paper towels.

COOKING

Preheat oven to 325°.

Heat oil to 380° in a deep fryer or large heavy kettle.

Kettle should be ⅓ full of oil.

If thermometer is not available, a small cube of bread dropped into oil will turn golden brown in approximately 1 minute when temperature is right for frying.

Place just enough potato strips in frying basket to cover bottom.

Immerse frying basket in hot oil and cook potato strips until golden, 3 to 5 minutes. Keep shaking strips while cooking so they won't stick.

Drain potato strips on paper towels.

Repeat until all potato strips have been cooked.

Keep potato strips warm in oven until the frying is completed.

SERVING

Sprinkle French fries with salt to taste, and serve from a paper napkin-lined bread basket or other interesting serving dish. (Use tongs for easy serving.)

Potatoes may also be served on the same plate as the beef or on individual side dishes.

Oven-Fried Potato Sticks

INGREDIENTS

4 mature baking potatoes,
   peeled and cut into strips

¼ cup corn or peanut oil
Salt

PREPARATION

Wash, peel, and cut raw potatoes into strips ¼–½-inch thick.

Soak potatoes in ice water for 10 minutes.

Drain potatoes and pat *thoroughly* dry on paper towels.

COOKING

Preheat oven to 450°.

Arrange potato strips in single layer on cookie tin or shallow baking dish.

Pour oil over potatoes and turn them with tongs to coat well.

Bake for 30 to 35 minutes, or until potato strips are golden brown.

Turn the strips several times during cooking to brown evenly.

Drain potato strips and pat dry on paper towel.

SERVING

Sprinkle potatoes with salt to taste and serve from a paper napkin-lined bread basket or other interesting serving dish. (Use tongs for easy serving.)

Potatoes may also be served on the same plate as the beef or on individual side dishes.

Steakhouse-Style Potato Chips

INGREDIENTS

4 medium-large baking potatoes, peeled and cut into paper-thin slices

Corn or peanut oil for deep-frying

Salt

PREPARATION

Wash, peel, and cut raw potatoes into paper-thin slices. (Use a vegetable peeler.)

Soak potato slices in ice water for 1 hour. Change water once during soaking.

Prepare boiling water in a large saucepan.

Remove potatoes from ice water, drain, and plunge into boiling water. Drain immediately.

Pat potato slices *thoroughly* dry on paper towels.

COOKING

Heat oil to 380° in a deep fryer or large heavy kettle. Kettle should be ⅓ full of oil.

If thermometer is not available, a small cube of bread dropped into oil will turn golden brown in approximately 1 minute when temperature is right for frying.

Place just enough potato slices in frying basket to cover bottom.

Immerse frying basket in hot oil and cook potato slices until golden.

Keep shaking the slices while cooking so they won't stick.

Drain potato slices on paper towels.

Repeat until all potato slices have been cooked.

SERVING

Sprinkle potato chips with salt before serving in an attractive bowl or paper napkin-lined bread basket.

INGREDIENTS

Skins from 4 baked potatoes, cut in half (see Baked Idaho Potato page 61)

¼ cup (½ stick) butter

¼ cup sharp grated Cheddar cheese (optional)

PREPARATION

Preheat oven to 500°.

Cut each potato in half and scoop out potato pulp.

Leave approximately ⅛ inch of potato on skin.

Cut each skin in half.

Set potatoes aside for another use (see Yorkshire Potato Pudding Puffs Page 67)

COOKING

Melt butter in a small saucepan.

Brush potato skins inside and out with butter.

Place skins on cookie sheet and bake for 12 minutes.

If using cheese, sprinkle over skins and place under broiler 4 inches away from heat for 2 minutes.

SERVING

Serve potato skins on a small platter.

Small bowls of sour cream, chive cream cheese, or other favorite topping may be served on the side with the skins (if Cheddar cheese is not used).

VEGETABLES

BEEF AND POTATOES are what steakhouses are all about, so occasionally you'll find that some restaurants don't pay much attention to the vegetables they serve beyond the token string beans or peas. Not so with these steakhouses and their vegetable fare! Your menu includes the steakhouse "standards"—French-Fried Onion Rings, Zucchini Chips, and Broiled Mushroom Caps. The string beans in the recipe here are served with an interesting deviled butter, and the fresh peas are cooked with mint.

During the past few years steakhouse owners have discovered that customers seem to like a creamed vegetable with their steak, and the consensus came up with spinach as number one. This is the reason you'll see creamed spinach on so many steakhouse menus.

Cooked radishes are a new and interesting vegetable getting a try-out, and they're delicious braised as in the following recipe, or boiled and mashed like a potato.

For your asparagus and other vegetables we've included an Emergency Hollandaise Sauce, just in case you need a quick substitute for the real thing.

BROILED MUSHROOM CAPS

BAKED TOMATO HALF

FRENCH-FRIED ONION RINGS

ZUCCHINI CHIPS

SKILLET-FRIED GREEN TOMATOES

BROILED GREEN PEPPER

ASPARAGUS WITH HOLLANDAISE SAUCE

BROCCOLI WITH LEMON DRESSING

CREAMED SPINACH

DEVILED GREEN BEANS

BRAISED RADISHES

GREEN PEAS WITH MINT

STEAMED BRUSSELS SPROUTS

Broiled Mushroom Caps

INGREDIENTS

12 large mushrooms

2 tablespoons (¼ stick) butter,
  divided into 12 pieces

Freshly ground black pepper
  (optional)

2 tablespoons (¼ stick) butter
  melted

PREPARATION

Wash mushrooms and pat dry with paper towel.

Remove stems and set aside for another use.

Arrange mushroom caps, tops down, in a shallow baking dish.

Place one piece of butter in each cap.

Sprinkle mushroom caps with freshly ground black pepper (optional).

COOKING

Preheat broiler.

Melt 2 tablespoons of butter in a small saucepan.

Brush mushroom caps with melted butter and place under broiler.

Broil for 5 to 7 minutes or until caps are tender.

SERVING

Serve immediately on the same plate as the beef. (1–3 mushroom caps may be placed on top of the beef, depending on the size of the steak)

Baked Tomato Half

INGREDIENTS

2 very large firm, ripe
tomatoes

1 small onion, minced

2 tablespoons (¼ stick) butter

¼ cup dry bread crumbs

1 tablespoon fresh minced
parsley

¼ teaspoon salt

Sprinkling of freshly ground
black pepper

PREPARATION

Wash tomatoes and remove stem ends.

Cut tomatoes in half and arrange in a shallow baking dish.

COOKING

Preheat oven to 400°.

In a small heavy skillet, sauté onion in butter until soft. Add bread
crumbs, parsley, salt, and pepper. Mix well.

Spread bread crumb mixture on tomato halves.

Bake for 25 minutes or until bread crumbs are nicely browned.

SERVING

Serve immediately on the same plate as the beef.

French-Fried Onion Rings

INGREDIENTS

3–4 large Bermuda onions
  sliced ¼-inch thick
¾ cup all-purpose flour
1 egg
½ teaspoon sugar

½ teaspoon salt
Corn or peanut oil for deep-
  frying

PREPARATION

Peel onions, and cut crosswise into slices ¼-inch thick. Separate slices into rings.

Refrigerate onion rings in ice water in a medium bowl for 1 hour.

Drain onion rings and pat dry on paper towels.

Beat flour, egg, sugar, and salt in a large bowl until smooth.

COOKING

Preheat oven to 325°.

Heat oil to 375° in a deep fryer or large heavy kettle.

Kettle should be ⅓ full of oil.

If thermometer is not available, a small cube of bread dropped into oil will turn golden brown in approximately 1 minute when temperature is right for frying.

Use a long-handled two-tine fork to dip onion rings into batter, 5 or 6 at a time.

Shake excess batter off over bowl.

Note: Onion rings may then be dipped in fine bread crumbs for a crustier coating.

Drop enough onion rings from fork into frying basket to cover bottom.

Immerse frying basket in hot oil and cook onion rings 1 to 2 minutes until golden brown.

Drain onion rings on paper towels.

Repeat until all onion rings have been cooked.

Keep onion rings warm in oven until the frying is completed.

SERVING

Serve as a side dish on individual plates or in a paper napkin-lined bread basket. Season at the table with salt to taste.

Zucchini Chips

INGREDIENTS

3 zucchini, 6–7 inches long
½ cup all-purpose flour
1 teaspoon salt
Generous sprinkling of
   freshly ground black
   pepper

2 eggs
1 tablespoon fresh lemon juice
1 cup fine dry bread crumbs
Corn or peanut oil for deep-
   frying

PREPARATION

Wash zucchini well under cold running water. Pat dry with paper towel. Trim ends of zucchini but do not peel.

Cut zucchini into slices ¼–½ inch thick.

Combine flour, salt, and pepper on a sheet of waxed paper.

Beat eggs with lemon juice in a medium bowl.

Spread bread crumbs on a sheet of waxed paper.

Coat zucchini slices with flour.

Dip slices in egg and then coat with bread crumbs.

COOKING

Preheat oven to 325°.

Heat oil to 365° in deep fryer or large heavy kettle.

Kettle should be ⅓ full of oil.

If thermometer is not available, a small cube of bread dropped into oil will turn golden brown in approximately 1 minute when temperature is right for frying.

Use tongs to place enough zucchini slices in frying basket to cover bottom.

Immerse frying basket in hot oil and cook zucchini slices approximately 1 minute, or until golden.

Drain zucchini slices on paper towels.

Repeat until all zucchini slices have been cooked.

Keep zucchini slices warm in oven until the frying is completed.

SERVING

Serve as a side dish on individual plates or in a paper napkin-lined bread basket.

Skillet-Fried Green Tomatoes

INGREDIENTS

4 medium-size green tomatoes (red tomatoes may also be used)

¾ cup fine corn bread crumbs (see Golden Corn Bread page 118)

½ teaspoon salt

Sprinkling of freshly ground black pepper

¼ cup corn oil

PREPARATION

Wash tomatoes and remove stem ends.

Cut tomatoes into slices ½ inch thick.

Prepare ¾ cup of fine corn bread crumbs from leftover corn bread.

Mix salt and pepper into corn bread crumbs and spread on wax paper.

Coat tomato slices on both sides with crumbs.

COOKING

Heat corn oil in a large heavy skillet until just sizzling. Reduce heat.

Lift tomato slices carefully into skillet with a spatula.

Fry slices on each side, turning once with spatula, until browned and crusty.

Drain tomato slices on paper towel.

SERVING

Serve immediately on individual side dishes.

Broiled Green Pepper

INGREDIENTS

4 medium-size green peppers
2 tablespoons (¼ stick) butter
Salt
Freshly ground black pepper

PREPARATION

Cut peppers lengthwise into quarters.

Trim off stem ends and remove seeds and fibrous portion of pepper.

Wash pepper slices inside and out.

Place peppers in a shallow baking dish.

COOKING

Broil peppers under moderate heat until edges begin to curl and peppers are just tender.

SERVING

Arrange pepper slices in an attractive serving dish, top with butter, and sprinkle with salt and freshly ground black pepper.

Asparagus with Hollandaise Sauce

INGREDIENTS

2 pounds deep green
  asparagus spears with
  tightly closed tips
¾ teaspoon salt

Hollandaise Sauce or
  Emergency Hollandaise
  Sauce (see below)
4 pimiento strips

PREPARATION

Wash asparagus spears in cool water with a soft brush.

Snap off any tough lower ends of spears.

Trim off scales if they have any trace of sand.

COOKING

Arrange asparagus spears in a single layer in a large heavy skillet.

Pour boiling water over asparagus to a depth of 1 inch.

Cover and cook asparagus in boiling water for 10 minutes, or until asparagus is tender. (Test lower part of a spear for tenderness with the sharp tip of a knife.)

Drain.

HOLLANDAISE SAUCE

INGREDIENTS

8 tablespoons (1 stick) butter
2 egg yolks
¼ teaspoon salt

Few grains cayenne
1 tablespoon fresh lemon juice
½ cup boiling water

COOKING

Melt butter in top part of double boiler over hot but not boiling water.

Whisk egg yolks into butter, one at a time, blending thoroughly.

Briskly whisk in salt, cayenne, and lemon juice.

Add boiling water a few drops at a time, whisking constantly.

Cook mixture until thickened, stirring all the while.

Use immediately.

EMERGENCY HOLLANDAISE SAUCE

INGREDIENTS

8 tablespoons (1 stick) butter
2 egg yolks
1–2 tablespoons fresh lemon
    juice

Salt
Few grains cayenne

COOKING

Place butter in a small saucepan over low heat.

Beat egg yolks slightly and add to butter.

Blend in lemon juice, salt, and cayenne.

Cook mixture over low heat, stirring constantly, until butter melts and sauce is thickened.

Use immediately.

SERVING

Arrange asparagus spears on individual serving plates.

Spoon hot Hollandaise Sauce over the top of spears.

Garnish with a pimiento strip and serve immediately.

Broccoli with Lemon Dressing

INGREDIENTS

**1 medium-size head purple-
  green broccoli**
Lemon Dressing (see below)
4 pimiento strips

PREPARATION

Wash broccoli under cold running water.

Trim off leaves and tough parts of stalks.

Cut 4 lengthwise gashes through bottom of stalks up to the head of broccoli to make 4 servings.

Soak broccoli in ice water for 10 minutes.

COOKING

Place broccoli in a steamer basket or pan over boiling water.

Cover and steam broccoli until tender.

LEMON DRESSING

INGREDIENTS

¼ cup olive oil
¼ cup fresh lemon juice
1–2 cloves garlic, crushed
½ teaspoon salt

Generous sprinkling of
  freshly ground black
  pepper

PREPARATION

Thoroughly mix all ingredients.

SERVING

Arrange hot broccoli on individual serving plates.

Spoon dressing over top of broccoli and garnish each serving with one pimiento strip. Serve immediately.

Creamed Spinach

INGREDIENTS

2 pounds young, fresh
  spinach
½ teaspoon salt
Sprinkling of freshly ground
  black pepper
¼ teaspoon nutmeg
1 tablespoon minced onion

1 thin slice garlic
2 tablespoons (¼ stick) butter
1 tablespoon all-purpose flour
½ cup milk
½ cup half-and-half
½ teaspoon sugar

PREPARATION

Pick over spinach leaves, discard coarse stems and any blemishes on leaves. Wash spinach quickly in warm water to release any sand, and rinse spinach several times under cold running water.

COOKING

Place spinach in a medium-size heavy saucepan with a tight-fitting lid.

Cover and cook spinach over low heat 10 to 15 minutes until tender. Do not add water.

Drain.

Chop spinach very fine and put in a medium bowl.

Sprinkle with salt, pepper, and nutmeg.

Sauté onion and garlic in butter in a medium-size heavy skillet until golden.

Stir in flour and cook over low heat until smooth.

Heat milk and half-and-half until just warm and stir warm milk and half-and-half into flour.

Add sugar and stir mixture until smooth and creamy.

Add spinach and cook for 3 to 5 minutes, stirring constantly.

SERVING

Serve immediately in small individual side bowls.

Deviled Green Beans

INGREDIENTS

1–1¼ pounds whole young
   green beans
3 tablespoons butter
½ teaspoon dry mustard
¾ teaspoon Worcestershire
   sauce

Few grains cayenne
Salt
Freshly ground black pepper

PREPARATION

Wash beans and trim off ends.

Cream butter in a small bowl and thoroughly blend in all other
ingredients.

COOKING

Place beans in 1 inch of boiling salted water in a large heavy saucepan.

Cover and cook 8 to 10 minutes until beans are tender-crisp.

Drain.

SERVING

Arrange beans on individual serving plates.

Serve immediately topped with seasoned butter.

Braised Radishes

INGREDIENTS

2 bunches firm, large red
    radishes trimmed and sliced

2 tablespoons (¼ stick) butter

½ teaspoon salt

2 tablespoons half-and-half

1 tablespoon fresh minced
    parsley

PREPARATION

Trim off tops and roots of radishes.

Wash radishes in cold water.

Slice.

COOKING

Cover sliced radishes with boiling water in a medium saucepan.

Cook for 10 minutes.

Drain.

Melt butter in the saucepan and add radishes.

Cook over low heat for 5 minutes.

Stir in salt, half-and-half, and parsley.

Cover and continue cooking radishes for 5 minutes.

SERVING

Serve immediately in small individual side bowls.

Green Peas with Mint

INGREDIENTS

2 pounds fresh peas in plump
    bright green pods
½ teaspoon salt
½ teaspoon fresh lemon juice
Pinch sugar
1 whole clove

4 sprigs fresh parsley
1 bay leaf
1 large mint leaf
3 tablespoons butter
1 teaspoon finely chopped
    fresh mint

PREPARATION

Wash pods and shell peas in a collander.

Pick over peas for blemishes. Save 2–3 pods.

COOKING

Place peas and 2–3 pods in ¼ cup of boiling salted water in a medium-size heavy saucepan.

Add lemon juice, sugar, clove, parsley, bay leaf, and mint leaf.

Cover tightly and simmer for 8 to 10 minutes until peas are tender and most of the water has evaporated.

Drain any water left in saucepan.

Discard pods and seasonings.

Add butter and chopped mint to peas and mix lightly.

SERVING

Serve immediately in small individual side bowls.

Steamed Brussels Sprouts

INGREDIENTS

1 pound Brussels sprouts, with tight-fitting outer leaves

1 tablespoon fresh lemon juice

2 tablespoons (¼ stick) butter

Salt

Freshly ground black pepper

PREPARATION

Wash Brussels sprouts under cold running water.

Cut off stems and remove any wilted leaves.

Soak Brussels sprouts in cold water for 10 minutes.

COOKING

Place Brussels sprouts in a steamer basket or pan over boiling water.

Cover and steam until tender.

SERVING

Arrange Brussels sprouts in small individual side bowls.

Sprinkle with lemon juice and top with butter.

Serve immediately, and season at the table with salt and pepper to taste.

THE SALAD BOWL

A PERFECT SALAD—the kind that the steakhouses serve—is easily put together if you select your greens and other vegetables with a critical eye for freshness and color as the restaurateurs do. You have to be both picky and demanding when selecting the "makings" for a salad that will look as good as it tastes. If your market lets vegetables get wilted and blemished, move on without delay to a store that prides itself on the kind of produce that looks as though it might have been just picked fresh from the garden. You can be sure that such a market will have a constant turnover.

Once you have the freshest of greens in hand, the *presentation* of your salad is the next step and it's an important one. Nothing short of droopy greens and disastrous dressings spoils the enjoyment of eating a salad more than large, unwieldy pieces of lettuce that refuse to stay on a fork. Rules of etiquette have decreed that it's proper to attack your salad with a knife, but greens and vegetables that have been torn, cut, chopped, and sliced into bite-size pieces are not only visually more appetizing, but they hold a salad dressing much better than a large leaf.

Take inventory of all your bowls and plates, and use them to best advantage in presenting your salad. Be imaginative and creative, and use dishes with an eye for color, size, and shape. A clear glass bowl, for instance, is ideal for serving the Super Bowl salad because it shows off the colorful variety of the vegetables. A fancy and not too large glass punch bowl will do double duty as a salad bowl for serving the elegant Caesar Salad. The brilliant red and purple of ripe beefsteak tomatoes and red onions set against a plain, stark white platter whet the appetite even before the vinaigrette dressing is drizzled on. A navy, black, or any dark color salad plate provides a dramatic contrast for the creamy white of Belgian endive and its matching Roquefort cream dressing. If you're serving salad as a first course, you can use anything from a shallow soup bowl to a large crystal goblet with all the possibilities in between! One steakhouse serves its coleslaw, cleverly garnished with a fringe of fresh parsley and a tomato flower, in hand-painted, small decorative flower pots that have become a favorite of collectors.

And finally, the freshest of greens and vegetables nicely prepared and artfully presented require a perfectly blended salad dressing. Your menu offers a collection of seventeen special "house" dressings, and salads that you can bring to the table just as they're served in the famous steakhouses.

SLICED TOMATOES AND ONIONS

SPINACH SALAD

CUCUMBERS AND ONIONS IN SOUR CREAM

SUPER BOWL

CAESAR SALAD

BELGIAN ENDIVE WITH ROQUEFORT CREAM DRESSING

WHITE CABBAGE COLESLAW

RED CABBAGE COLESLAW

PIMIENTOS, ANCHOVIES, AND CAPERS ON CHOPPED
   LETTUCE

THREE-GREENS SALAD WITH THOUSAND ISLAND
   DRESSING

DIETERS' SPECIAL SALAD BOWL WITH SIX-CALORIE
   DRESSING

THE FIVE "HOUSE" FRENCH DRESSINGS

   NUMBER ONE

   NUMBER TWO

   NUMBER THREE

   NUMBER FOUR

   NUMBER FIVE

MAYONNAISE

SIX-CALORIE DRESSING

GARNISHES FOR SALADS

Sliced Tomatoes and Onions

INGREDIENTS

2 large firm ripe beefsteak
tomatoes, sliced ½-inch
thick

1 large red onion, sliced ¼-
inch thick

Salt

¼ cup olive oil

2 tablespoons cider vinegar

Freshly ground black pepper

2 tablespoons fresh minced
parsley

PREPARATION

Wash tomatoes and remove stem ends.

Cut tomatoes into slices ½-inch thick.

Peel onions and cut into slices ¼-inch thick.

Alternate tomato and onion slices in a single layer on an attractive
serving platter.

Sprinkle with salt.

Thoroughly mix oil and vinegar.

Drizzle over tomato and onion slices.

Sprinkle with pepper and parsley.

Cover tomatoes and onions with plastic wrap and refrigerate for 1
hour.

SERVING

Serve at the table on individual salad plates.

Spinach Salad

INGREDIENTS

½ pound raw young fresh spinach, torn into bite-size pieces

1 large ripe tomato, coarsely chopped

1 small stalk celery, thinly sliced.

1 large egg, hard-cooked and cut into quarters

1 small onion, minced.

½ cup Number One French dressing (see recipe page 109) or salad dressing of your choice

PREPARATION

Pick over spinach leaves, discarding any with coarse stems and blemishes.

Wash spinach quickly in warm water to release any sand.

Rinse spinach several times under cold running water.

Drain, and pat dry with paper towel.

Wrap spinach in plastic and chill for 1–2 hours.

Wash tomato and remove stem end.

Wash celery and trim off leaves.

Chill tomato and celery for 1–2 hours.

Cover egg with cold water in a small saucepan.

Bring water to a boil.

Remove the saucepan from heat and cover with a tight-fitting lid.

Let the egg stand for at least 1 hour.

Run egg under cold water.

Remove shell and chill.

Tear spinach into bite-size pieces with your fingers, or shred with kitchen shears.

Chop tomato coarsely.

Peel onion and mince.

Cut celery stalk into thin slices.

Combine spinach, tomato, onion, and celery, in a large attractive salad bowl.

Pour salad dressing over all and toss lightly until vegetables are well coated. Use a little extra dressing if necessary.

Slice egg into quarters.

SERVING

Serve at the table on individual salad plates.

Garnish each serving with a quarter of hard-cooked egg.

Cucumbers and Onions in Sour Cream

INGREDIENTS

2 firm medium cucumbers

1 teaspoon salt

¾ cup sour cream

1 tablespoon cider vinegar, or to taste

¼ teaspoon sugar

Sprinkling white pepper

1 small onion

1 tablespoon fresh minced parsley

PREPARATION

Wash and peel cucumbers.

Cut cucumbers into paper-thin slices (use a vegetable peeler) and place in a shallow serving dish.

Sprinkle with salt.

Cover dish with plastic, and chill cucumbers for 1 hour.

Drain cucumbers and pat dry with paper towel.

Combine sour cream, vinegar, sugar, and pepper in a small bowl and blend well.

Peel onion, and cut into thin slices.

Arrange cucumber and onion slices in shallow serving dish.

Add sour cream dressing and mix lightly but well.

Cover with plastic and chill for 2 hours.

SERVING

Sprinkle parsley over top of cucumber and onion slices.

Serve at the table in small individual side bowls.

Super Bowl

INGREDIENTS

½ medium head lettuce, coarsely chopped

4 medium radishes, thinly sliced

1 small carrot, thinly sliced

1 small stalk celery, minced (trim off leaves)

1 small onion, minced

½ small green pepper, minced

1 medium tomato, coarsely chopped

4–5 pitted black olives, thinly sliced

1 tablespoon fresh minced parsley

1 medium clove garlic, cut in half

½ cup Number Four French dressing (see recipe, page 110) or salad dressing of your choice

PREPARATION

Chill all vegetables except garlic.

Rub a large wooden salad bowl well with garlic halves and discard garlic.

Wash, trim, and prepare all vegetables as described in the ingredients list.

Arrange vegetables in the garlic-seasoned salad bowl.

Pour dressing over all and toss lightly until vegetables are well coated. Use a little extra dressing if necessary.

SERVING

Serve at the table on individual salad plates or in small bowls.

Caesar Salad

INGREDIENTS

1 clove garlic, cut in half

1 medium head dark green romaine lettuce, torn into 2-inch pieces

1 teaspoon salt

¼ teaspoon dry mustard

Generous sprinkling of freshly ground black pepper

Few drops Worcestershire sauce

4–6 anchovy fillets, cut into small pieces

6 tablespoons olive oil

3 tablespoons wine vinegar

1 tablespoon fresh lemon juice

1 egg

1 cup toasted croutons

3 tablespoons freshly grated Parmesan cheese

PREPARATION

Rub a large wooden salad bowl well with garlic halves and discard garlic.

Trim ends and pick over lettuce leaves.

Separate leaves and wash them individually under cold running water. Pat dry with paper towel.

Wrap lettuce in plastic and chill for 1 hour.

Tear lettuce into approximately 2-inch pieces into the garlic-seasoned salad bowl.

Sprinkle with salt, mustard, pepper, and Worcestershire sauce.

Cut anchovy fillets into small pieces and add to salad bowl.

Thoroughly mix oil, vinegar, and lemon juice in a small bowl.

Pour mixture over lettuce and anchovies.

Crack egg and drop from its shell onto the salad.

Sprinkle croutons and Parmesan cheese over all.

Note: Use packaged croutons or make them yourself (recipe page 123).

Toss lightly but thoroughly until lettuce leaves are well coated with dressing.

SERVING

Serve immediately at the table on individual salad plates or in small bowls.

Belgian Endive with Roquefort Cream Dressing

INGREDIENTS

4 creamy white stalks Belgian endive 4–6 inches long

2 tablespoon cream cheese, softened

1–1½ ounces Roquefort cheese, crumbled

2 tablespoons heavy cream

2 tablespoons plus 2 teaspoons mayonnaise (see Mayonnaise, page 110)

1 teaspoon fresh lemon juice

1 teaspoon wine vinegar

Paprika

PREPARATION

Chill four salad plates.

Wash endive stalks under cool running water.

Drain, and pat dry gently with paper towel.

Trim base of each stalk

Cut stalks in half lengthwise.

Arrange endive on salad plates.

Combine cream cheese and Roquefort in a small bowl and blend thoroughly until smooth.

Stir in cream, mayonnaise, lemon juice, and vinegar.

Beat until well blended and creamy.

SERVING

Spoon Roquefort dressing over endive.

Sprinkle with paprika before serving.

Note: For best taste and color, endive should be used within one or two days after purchasing. Wrap tightly in plastic and refrigerate until ready to use.

White Cabbage Coleslaw

INGREDIENTS

½ small head cabbage, finely shredded

½ small onion, minced

½ cup mayonnaise (see Mayonnaise page 110)

2 tablespoons cider vinegar

1 teaspoon salt

½ teaspoon sugar

Sprinkling of white pepper

Paprika

PREPARATION

Wash cabbage and remove any blemished outer leaves and the core.

Shred cabbage very fine into a medium bowl.

Mince onion.

Add all ingredients except paprika to cabbage.

Toss coleslaw lightly but well.

Cover and chill for 1 hour.

SERVING

Serve coleslaw in small individual salad bowls.

Sprinkle with paprika before serving.

Red Cabbage Coleslaw

INGREDIENTS

½ small red cabbage, finely shredded

1 small carrot finely shredded

½ small red onion, minced

¼ teaspoon celery seed

½ cup Number Three French dressing (see recipe, page 109)

PREPARATION

Wash cabbage and remove any blemished outer leaves and the core.

Shred cabbage very fine into a medium bowl.

Wash and peel carrot and cut off top. Shred carrot very fine into cabbage.

Mince onion.

Add onion and celery seed.

Pour dressing over all.

Toss coleslaw lightly but well.

Cover and chill for 1 hour.

SERVING

Serve coleslaw in small individual salad bowls.

Pimientos, Anchovies, and Capers on Chopped Lettuce

INGREDIENTS

¼ cup corn oil
2 tablespoons cider vinegar
1 clove garlic, minced
1 teaspoon fresh minced parsley
½ teaspoon salt

4 large (canned) pimientos
8 lettuce leaves
8 flat anchovies
1 heaping teaspoon capers
Freshly ground black pepper

PREPARATION

Combine oil, vinegar, garlic, parsley, and salt in a small jar with a tight-fitting lid. Shake well and refrigerate for 1 hour.

Drain pimientos and chill for 1 hour.

Wash lettuce leaves, drain, and pat dry with paper towel.

Chop lettuce coarsely.

Arrange a bed of lettuce on individual salad plates.

Place a pimiento on top of lettuce.

Crisscross 2 anchovies over each pimiento.

Top with a sprinkling of capers.

Drizzle oil and vinegar over all.

Sprinkle with freshly ground black pepper and serve immediately.

Three-Greens Salad with Thousand Island Dressing

INGREDIENTS

1 bunch arugula, torn into small pieces

4 large leaves radicchio, torn into small pieces

1 head Bibb lettuce, torn into small pieces

1 egg, hard-cooked and finely chopped

½ cup mayonnaise (see Mayonnaise page 110)

1 tablespoon chili sauce

1 teaspoon cider vinegar

1 tablespoon heavy cream

1 tablespoon minced celery

Salt

PREPARATION

Pick over greens, and discard stems and blemishes on leaves.

Wash greens well under cold running water.

Shake off excess water and pat dry with paper towel.

Wrap greens in plastic and chill for 1 hour.

Cover egg with cold water in a small saucepan.

Bring water to a boil.

Remove the saucepan from heat and cover with a tight-fitting lid.

Let the egg stand for at least 1 hour.

Run egg under cold water.

Remove shell and chill.

Finely chop egg in a small bowl.

Combine egg, mayonnaise, chili sauce, vinegar, cream, and celery.

Mix well and add salt to taste.

Tear greens into small pieces with your fingers.

SERVING

Arrange greens on individual salad plates.

Spoon dressing over top and serve immediately.

Dieters' Special Salad Bowl with Six-Calorie Dressing

INGREDIENTS

Greens of your choice (or all three below)

1 bunch escarole, torn into small pieces

1 head Boston lettuce, torn into small pieces

1 bunch chicory, torn into small pieces

Six-Calorie Dressing (see recipe page 111)

PREPARATION

Pick over greens and discard ends, coarse pieces, and blemishes.

Wash greens well under cold running water.

Shake off excess water and pat dry with paper towel.

Wrap greens in plastic and chill for 1 hour.

Tear greens into bite-size pieces with your fingers, or shred with kitchen shears.

SERVING

Arrange greens on individual salad plates.

Spoon 1 tablespoon (approximately 6 calories) dressing over each serving.

The Five "House" French Dressings

PREPARATION

Combine all ingredients for each French dressing in a glass jar with a tight-fitting lid.

Shake well and chill (unless otherwise specified).

Keep dressings refrigerated, and shake well each time before using.

The dressings are numbered for easy reference, and not in order of quality.

NUMBER ONE

¾ cup olive oil

¼ cup cider vinegar

1 teaspoon salt

1 teaspoon sugar

½ teaspoon paprika

¼ teaspoon dry mustard

Sprinkling of freshly ground
   black pepper

Note: Recipe makes 1 cup.

NUMBER TWO

½ cup olive oil

¼ cup red wine vinegar

1 teaspoon salt

Sprinkling of freshly ground
   black pepper

¼ cup tomato ketchup

1 tablespoon sugar, or to taste

1 teaspoon minced onion

½ teaspoon celery seed

Note: Recipe makes 1 cup. Use within 24 hours.

NUMBER THREE

¼ cup corn oil

¼ cup olive oil

2 tablespoons cider vinegar

2 tablespoons fresh lemon
   juice

½ teaspoon salt

¼ teaspoon dry mustard

¼ teaspoon paprika

Note: Recipe makes ¾ cup.

NUMBER FOUR

2 tablespoons tarragon
  vinegar

¼ cup plus 2 tablespoons
  walnut oil

½ teaspoon salt

Sprinkling of white pepper

¼ teaspoon prepared mustard

¼ teaspoon dry mustard

½ teaspoon each of fresh
  minced basil, parsley,
  rosemary, and chervil

Note: Recipe makes approximately ½ cup. Use immediately, and
  do not refrigerate or store.

NUMBER FIVE

3 tablespoons honey

1 tablespoon tomato ketchup

½ teaspoon dry mustard

1 teaspoon prepared
  horseradish

1 teaspoon salt

¼ teaspoon celery seed

1 small clove garlic, cut in half

2 tablespoons cider vinegar

½ cup corn oil

2 tablespoons fresh lemon
  juice

Note: Refrigerate for 12 hours. Remove garlic clove before using.
  Recipe makes 1 cup.

Mayonnaise

INGREDIENTS

2 egg yolks

½ teaspoon dry mustard

Dash cayenne

½ teaspoon salt

½ teaspoon fresh lemon juice

1 cup olive oil

1 tablespoon cider vinegar

½ tablespoon tarragon vinegar

2 tablespoons fresh lemon
  juice

PREPARATION

Have *all* ingredients at room temperature.

Warm mixing bowl with hot water, and dry.

Whisk egg yolks, mustard, cayenne, salt, and ½ teaspoon lemon juice in a medium bowl until stiff.

Beat in ½ cup oil, at first very slowly drop by drop, and then a few drops at a time.

Keep the mixture stiff.

Mix vinegars and remaining lemon juice in a cup.

Slowly alternate the remaining ½ cup of oil and vinegar-lemon juice *drop by drop* into the bowl, whisking constantly.

The mayonnaise will separate if oil is added too quickly.

Keep mixture smooth and well blended.

Note: If mayonnaise should become too thick, whisk in a few drops of cream. Recipe makes approximately 1¼ cups. Refrigerate mayonnaise, tightly covered, until ready to use.

Six-Calorie Dressing

INGREDIENTS

¾ cup vegetable juice (see Vegetable Juice Cocktail page 19)

2 teaspoons cider vinegar

1 teaspoon fresh lemon juice

½ teaspoon prepared mustard

½ teaspoon Worcestershire sauce

Dash paprika

1 small clove garlic, minced

1 teaspoon fresh minced parsley

Note: Recipe makes approximately ¾ cup, 6 calories per tablespoon. Keep dressing refrigerated, and shake well each time before using. Use within 2 to 3 days for best flavor.

Garnishes for Salads

TOMATO FLOWER

Cut skin and approximately ⅛ inch of pulp on a small firm tomato into 4–6 "petals," within ½ inch of bottom of tomato.

Trim off stem end.

Loosen petals carefully, and pull outward from pulp, leaving round center intact.

CUCUMBER ACCORDIANS

Cut 2-inch pieces from a small cucumber.

Slice cucumber piece approximately ⅛-inch thick, but not all the way through.

Seed cucumber and spread slices.

Pull fresh parsley sprigs through ring of slices.

LEMON UMBRELLAS

Cut ¼-inch slices of lemon in half to resemble umbrella tops.

Use pimiento strip and turn up bottom for "handle" of umbrella.

BLACK OR GREEN PITTED OLIVES

Pull a carrot strip, fresh parsley sprig, or piece of anchovy through center of large pitted olives.

CARROT CURLS

Pare paper-thin slices of carrot lengthwise with vegetable peeler.

Roll up slices and secure with a toothpick.

Soak in ice water for 1 hour.

Remove toothpicks before garnishing.

CARROT FLOWER

Arrange thin slices of carrot cut crosswise around a small black or green olive center.

Use sprig of fresh parsley for leaves and stem.

VEGETABLE CHAINS:

Cucumber

Peel and seed a small cucumber, and cut into thin slices.

Cut each slice on one side and loop one cucumber slice over another to form a chain.

Red and White Onion

Cut one small white and one small red onion into thin slices.

Separate slices and cut each slice on one side.

Alternate one slice of red and one slice of white onion over another to form a chain.

Green Pepper

Cut pepper crosswise into thin slices, and seed.

Trim off stem end.

Cut each slice on one side and loop one pepper slice over another to form a chain.

CONFETTI

Grate carrot, mince fresh parsley, mince hard-cooked egg yolk, and sprinkle over salad like confetti.

THE BREAD BASKET

A BOUNTIFUL bread basket on the table is a tempting sight, especially when the bread and crackers are all home-made. It takes only the slightest extra bit of effort to turn out any one of the recipes that follow.

The bread basket should have variety, so be sure to include a mixture of textures and tastes like Onion Biscuits, Savory Crisp Ribbons, a small corn bread and Cheddar Squares. One perfect popover should be served alone on an attractive butter plate, and of course a crusty brown garlic bread mixes with no other loaf!

With soup, Chopped Chicken Livers, and Roquefort Cheese Mousse, old-fashioned Home-Made Soda Crackers are a special treat. And for another special treat, take a few extra minutes to whip up your own sweet or lightly salted butter, and season it if you like. Press softened butter into small candy or cookie molds that have an interesting shape (leaf, crescent, triangle, etc.) and unmold individual servings of the home-made butter onto butter plates. The shaped butters may also be placed on crushed ice in a silver or other fancy small bowl. When you're serving a *big* steak and *big* portions, a whole one-pound bar of butter placed on the table is impressive, in keeping with the mood of the meal.

Line the bread basket with a big snowy white cloth napkin, and pull it over the top of the bread and crackers to keep them warm during the meal. Use a big, thick paper dinner napkin to wrap the garlic bread.

ONION BISCUITS

TOASTED GARLIC BREAD

GOLDEN CORN BREAD

SAVORY CRISP RIBBONS

POPOVERS

CHEDDAR SQUARES

HOME-MADE SODA CRACKERS

CROUTONS

Onion Biscuits

INGREDIENTS

1 cup all-purpose flour
1½ teaspoons baking powder
½ teaspoon salt

2⅔ tablespoons corn oil
⅓ cup milk
1 small onion, minced

PREPARATION

Preheat oven to 475°.

Sift flour, baking powder, and salt together in a medium bowl.

Pour oil and milk together into flour.

Stir in onion and mix well with a fork until batter cleans the sides of bowl.

Drop batter from a spoon into an 8-cup ungreased muffin tin.

Bake biscuits for 10 to 12 minutes.

SERVING

Serve biscuits hot from the oven in a bread basket lined and covered with a large white cloth napkin.

Toasted Garlic Bread

INGREDIENTS

1 medium loaf French or
   Italian bread
8 tablespoons (1 stick) butter

1–2 large cloves garlic, minced

PREPARATION

Preheat oven to 350°.

Cut bread diagonally, ¾ of the way through, into 1-inch-thick slices.

Melt butter with garlic in a small saucepan.

Separate bread slices and pour a little garlic butter between each slice.

Brush top and sides of bread with garlic butter.

Wrap bread in foil.

Place on rack in oven for 20 minutes, or until bread is heated through and browned on top.

SERVING

Serve bread hot from the oven in a bread basket long enough to hold the whole loaf in one piece.

Line and cover the basket with a large white paper napkin.

Golden Corn Bread

INGREDIENTS

¾ cup all-purpose flour
1½ teaspoons baking powder
1 tablespoon brown sugar
1 teaspoon salt
1¼ cups yellow stone-ground
  corn meal

1 egg
2 tablespoons (¼ stick) butter
¾ cup buttermilk

PREPARATION

Preheat oven to 425°.

Generously butter a heavy 9-inch square baking pan.

Heat empty pan in oven until sizzling hot.

Sift flour, baking powder, sugar, and salt together in a medium bowl.

Add corn meal.

Beat egg in a small bowl.

Melt 2 tablespoons butter in a small saucepan.

Beat butter into egg with ¾ cup of buttermilk.

Stir buttermilk mixture briskly into corn meal, and blend well.

Pour corn meal batter into hot pan.

Bake for 20 to 25 minutes.

SERVING

Cut corn bread into squares or bars and serve immediately in a bread basket lined and covered with a large white cloth napkin.

Note: Recipe makes 12 pieces of corn bread. Wrap leftover corn bread in foil.

Savory Crisp Ribbons

INGREDIENTS

1 cup all-purpose flour
½ teaspoon salt
⅔ cup shortening
6 ounces cream cheese

Salt
Your choice of celery, poppy, sesame, or caraway seeds

PREPARATION

Preheat oven to 375°.

Sift flour and salt together in a medium bowl.

Cut in shortening and cream cheese with two table knives or pastry blender.

Mix thoroughly to form dough.

Roll dough out on a lightly floured board with a rolling pin to approximately ⅛-inch thickness.

Sprinkle dough lightly with salt and your choice of seeds.

Note: If using caraway seeds, mix 1 tablespoon in with the dough before rolling.

Cut dough into strips 3 inches long and 1 inch wide.

Bake strips on a large cookie sheet for approximately 6 minutes, or until lightly browned.

SERVING

Serve ribbons in a bread basket lined and covered with a large white cloth napkin.

Note: Recipe makes approximately 24 ribbons. Store ribbons in refrigerator, wrapped in foil.

Popovers

INGREDIENTS

1 egg   **½ cup all-purpose flour**
½ cup cold milk   **¼ teaspoon salt**

PREPARATION

Beat egg and milk well in a small bowl.

Sift flour and salt into egg.

Beat mixture until smooth and creamy.

Generously butter a 6-cup muffin tin.

Spoon batter into muffin tin, filling each cup ⅔ full.

Place muffin tin in cold oven.

Heat oven to 450°.

Bake for 30 minutes until popovers are golden brown and puffy.

SERVING

Serve popovers hot from the oven on individual butter plates.

Cheddar Squares

INGREDIENTS

4 slices fresh bread
2 eggs
½ teaspoon salt
2 tablespoons (¼ stick) butter

1 cup sharp Cheddar cheese,
  grated
Butter

PREPARATION

Preheat oven to 350°.

Cut each slice of bread into four cubes approximately 2 inches square.

Beat eggs and salt lightly in a medium bowl.

Spread grated cheese on a sheet of wax paper.

Dip both sides of each bread square into egg mixture and then into grated cheese.

Melt butter in a small saucepan.

Lightly butter a cookie sheet.

Place squares on cookie sheet and bake until cheese is melted and squares are lightly browned.

SERVING

Serve cheese squares in a bread basket lined and covered with a large white cloth napkin.

Home-Made Soda Crackers

INGREDIENTS

2 cups all-purpose flour

¼ teaspoon baking soda

½ teaspoon salt

8 tablespoons (1 stick) butter

¼ cup plus 2 tablespoons buttermilk

PREPARATION

Preheat oven to 400°.

Sift flour, baking soda, and salt together in a medium bowl.

Cut butter into flour with two table knives, a pastry blender, or your fingers.

Work lightly until mixture is coarse and mealy.

Add buttermilk and thoroughly mix into a stiff dough.

Roll dough out on a lightly floured board with a rolling pin. Keep turning dough over and rolling out until very stiff.

Roll dough out paper-thin.

Cut dough into squares and prick squares with a fork.

Lift squares with a spatula onto a large cookie sheet.

Bake until edges of squares are lightly browned.

Remove from oven and set aside to cool.

SERVING

Serve crackers with assorted rolls and bread sticks in a bread basket lined and covered with a large white cloth napkin.

Note: Recipe makes 25–30 crackers. Store crackers in a tightly covered tin.

PREPARATION

Preheat oven to 375°.

Lightly butter 3–4 slices of white or wheat bread.

Cut bread into approximately ½-inch cubes.

Place bread cubes on a cookie sheet.

Bake until nicely browned.

Set croutons aside to cool.

SERVING

Serve with Caesar Salad (see page 102) and with soups.

Note: Recipe makes approximately 1 cup.

HOME-MADE SWEET CREAM BUTTER

SEASONED BUTTERS:

   Lightly Salted

   Parsley

   Chive

   Herb

   Dill

   Onion

   Garlic

   Lemon

   Deviled

Home-Made Sweet Cream Butter

INGREDIENTS

1 cup heavy cream
¼ cup cold water
3 ice cubes
Yellow food color (optional)

PREPARATION

Pour heavy cream into blender.

Blend at high speed for a few seconds until smooth.

Add water and ice cubes.

Blend at high speed until butter particles float on top.

Strain.

OR

Beat heavy cream with electric mixer in a medium bowl until liquid separates from butter. Do not add water or ice cubes.

Strain off liquid.

Knead the butter with a wooden spoon until all excess liquid is pressed out.

Press the butter into an attractive serving dish or mold.

Cover and refrigerate until ready to use.

Yellow food color may be added to butter (optional).

Note: Recipe makes ⅓ cup of butter.

Seasoned Butters

Into ⅓ cup of softened Home-Made Sweet Cream Butter mix:

1 teaspoon salt, or to taste	**LIGHTLY SALTED BUTTER**
1 tablespoon fresh minced parsley	**PARSLEY BUTTER**
1 tablespoon fresh minced chives	**CHIVE BUTTER**
1 teaspoon fresh minced parsley 1 teaspoon fresh chives, minced	**HERB BUTTER**
1 tablespoon fresh minced dill	**DILL BUTTER**
1 teaspoon minced onion	**ONION BUTTER**
1 medium clove minced garlic	**GARLIC BUTTER**
½ teaspoon fresh lemon juice	**LEMON BUTTER**
½ teaspoon dry mustard ¾ teaspoon Worcestershire sauce Few grains cayenne	**DEVILED BUTTER**

Note: Use seasoned butters within 24 hours.

DESSERTS

SWEETS USED to be served *before* the meal, but happily they're now our last course, and what better ending for a perfect steak dinner than these twelve desserts. There's something here for everyone, and you can choose from a simple baked custard to a sinfully rich Chocolate Chiffon Pie with Whipped Cream. If you decide on one of the home-made ice creams, there's even a real old-fashioned hot fudge sauce to go on top.

You don't need to have a sweet tooth to be tempted by this collection of sweets, and just for tonight no one is allowed to think about or count calories!

If you really haven't saved enough room for dessert, you can console yourself with a home-made after-dinner mint.

OLD-FASHIONED BAKED CUSTARD CUP

COFFEE RUM ICE CREAM

FROZEN VANILLA MERINGUE CUSTARD

BUTTER PECAN ICE CREAM

HOT CHOCOLATE FUDGE SAUCE

TRIPLE-FRUIT SHERBET

LEMON CREAM

CHOCOLATE CHIFFON PIE WITH WHIPPED CREAM

CREAM CHEESECAKE WITH CINNAMON-BUTTER-CRUMB
  CRUST

BUTTERSCOTCH NINE O'CLOCKS

POOR-BOY BRANDIED PEACHES

ROQUEFORT CHEESE MOUSSE WITH ASSORTED
  CRACKERS

AFTER-DINNER PEPPERMINT WAFERS

Old-Fashioned Baked Custard Cup

INGREDIENTS

3 eggs
¼ teaspoon salt
⅓ cup sugar
3 cups milk

½ teaspoon pure vanilla
    extract
Nutmeg

PREPARATION

Beat eggs slightly with salt and sugar in a medium bowl.

COOKING

Place a shallow pan of hot water on middle rack of oven.

Preheat oven to 350°.

Scald milk (heat just until tiny bubbles form on top) in top part of double boiler over boiling water. Do not let top pan touch boiling water in pan below.

Add milk *slowly* to eggs, stirring constantly.

Stir in vanilla.

Pour mixture into individual custard or decorative ovenproof cups.

Sprinkle with nutmeg.

Place cups in pan of hot water in oven.

Bake for 25 to 30 minutes, or until a knife inserted at the edge of cup comes out clean.

Chill.

SERVING

Serve chilled custard cups on small individual serving plates.

Coffee Rum Ice Cream

INGREDIENTS

½ cup strong black coffee, chilled

⅔ cup sweetened condensed milk

2 tablespoons rum

1 cup heavy cream

PREPARATION

Thoroughly blend coffee, condensed milk, and rum in a medium bowl.

Empty ice cube tray and pour coffee mixture into tray.

Cover with foil and freeze for approximately 2 hours, or until ice crystals begin to form around sides of tray.

Whip cream until thick enough to form a soft peak.

Fold whipped cream into mixture in tray.

Cover with foil and freeze for approximately 1 hour, until coffee mixture is half-frozen but still mushy.

Scrape sides and bottom of tray and spoon mixture back into bowl.

Beat until smooth and creamy, but not melted.

Return coffee cream mixture to ice cube tray and cover with foil.

Freeze until firm.

SERVING

Serve in decorative glass bowls or dessert dishes.

Note: Recipe provides one or two extra servings.

Frozen Vanilla Meringue Custard

INGREDIENTS

2 egg whites
Sprinkling salt,
    approximately ⅛ teaspoon
¼ cup sugar

1 cup heavy cream
½ teaspoon pure vanilla
    extract

PREPARATION

Beat egg whites with salt in a medium bowl until almost stiff.
Add sugar gradually, and continue beating to form a stiff meringue.

Whip cream with vanilla in a small bowl until thick enough to form
a soft peak.

Fold whipped cream into meringue.

Empty ice cube tray and pour meringue mixture into tray.

Freeze mixture until firm.

Do not stir.

SERVING

Serve in parfait or champagne glasses.

Note: Recipe provides one or two extra servings.

Butter Pecan Ice Cream

INGREDIENTS

½ cup sugar
½ teaspoon salt
1⅓ cups milk
2 tablespoons (¼ stick) butter
1 cup pecans, coarsely chopped

2 eggs, separated
1 cup heavy cream
1 teaspoon pure vanilla extract
4 large pecans

PREPARATION

Dissolve sugar and salt in milk.

Melt butter in a small heavy skillet.

Brown chopped pecans in butter and set aside to cool.

Beat egg whites in a small bowl until stiff but not dry.

Beat egg yolks in a small bowl until thick and creamy.

Whip cream in a large bowl until thick enough to form a soft peak.

Add vanilla to whipped cream, and fold in milk, pecans, egg whites, and egg yolks.

Empty ice cube tray and pour pecan mixture into tray.

Freeze, stirring every 30 minutes, for approximately 2 hours, or until mixture holds its shape.

Continue freezing until firm.

SERVING

Serve in parfait glasses and top each serving with a pecan.

Note: Recipe provides one or two extra servings.

Hot Chocolate Fudge Sauce

INGREDIENTS

1 tablespoon butter

2 ounces unsweetened chocolate

½ cup boiling water

1 cup sugar

2 tablespoons corn syrup

1 teaspoon pure vanilla extract

PREPARATION

Melt butter in top part of double boiler over boiling water.

Do not let top saucepan touch boiling water in saucepan below.

Add chocolate and stir until melted.

Slowly stir in boiling water.

Mix in sugar and corn syrup and blend well.

Remove top saucepan and place over direct heat.

Cover.

Let chocolate sauce boil gently for 2 to 3 minutes.

Uncover saucepan and reduce heat.

Simmer chocolate sauce for 5 minutes.

Stir in vanilla.

SERVING

Spoon generously over the ice cream of your choice.

Triple-Fruit Sherbet

INGREDIENTS

1 ripe banana, mashed
½ cup freshly squeezed
   orange juice with pulp
¼ cup fresh lemon juice

¾ cup sugar
Sprinkling salt,
   approximately ⅛ teaspoon
1 cup evaporated milk, chilled

PREPARATION

Mash banana in a medium bowl.

Thoroughly mix in orange juice, 2 tablespoons of the lemon juice, sugar, and salt.

Empty ice cube tray and pour fruit mixture into tray.

Cover with foil and freeze, stirring every 30 minutes to keep mixture slushy, for approximately 2 hours.

Whip chilled milk in a small bowl until light and fluffy.

Add remaining lemon juice.

Continue beating milk until stiff.

Fold whipped milk into fruit mixture.

Do not stir.

Cover with foil.

Freeze mixture until firm.

SERVING

Serve sherbet in champagne or favorite stem glasses.

Lemon Cream

INGREDIENTS

2 eggs
½ cup sugar
½ cup light corn syrup
1 cup milk

1 cup half-and-half
¼ cup fresh lemon juice
1 teaspoon grated lemon rind

PREPARATION

Beat eggs briskly in a medium bowl until thick and creamy.

Add sugar gradually, and continue beating until mixture is very thick.

Blend in all other ingredients and mix well.

Empty ice cube tray and pour in lemon mixture.

Cover with foil.

Freeze for approximately 2 hours, until lemon mixture is half-frozen but still mushy.

Spoon mixture back into bowl.

Beat until light and creamy.

Return lemon cream to ice cube tray and cover with foil.

Freeze until firm.

SERVING

Serve in parfait glasses or goblets.

Chocolate Chiffon Pie with Whipped Cream

INGREDIENTS

1 tablespoon unflavored gelatin

¼ cup cold water

½ cup boiling water

2 ounces unsweetened chocolate

4 eggs

1 cup sugar

¼ teaspoon salt

1 teaspoon pure vanilla extract

9-inch single-crust pie shell of your choice

½ cup heavy cream

PREPARATION

Soften gelatin in cold water for 5 minutes.

Mix boiling water with chocolate in a medium bowl.

Blend until smooth.

Add gelatin to chocolate and stir until dissolved.

Separate eggs. Set whites aside in a medium bowl and beat egg yolks slightly in a small bowl.

Add yolks, ½ cup of sugar, salt, and vanilla to chocolate.

Thoroughly beat chocolate mixture until smooth.

Set aside until cool and mixture begins to thicken.

Beat egg whites until foamy.

Beat remaining ½ cup of sugar gradually into egg whites.

Fold into chocolate mixture.

Pour chocolate mixture into pie shell.

Chill in refrigerator until firm.

When pie is firm, whip cream in a small bowl until thick enough to form a soft peak.

SERVING

Slice pie and serve on small attractive plates.

Pass a bowl of whipped cream for diners to help themselves, or whipped cream may be spread over top of pie before serving.

Cream Cheesecake With Cinnamon-Butter-Crumb Crust

INGREDIENTS

8 tablespoons (1 stick) butter

2 cups fine zwieback crumbs

½ cup sugar

1 teaspoon cinnamon

1 pound plus 1 tablespoon
   cream cheese, softened

½ cup sugar

2 tablespoons flour

¼ teaspoon salt

4 eggs

1 teaspoon pure vanilla extract

1 cup heavy cream

PREPARATION

Melt butter in a small saucepan.

Thoroughly mix 1¼ cups of crumbs with melted butter, sugar, and cinnamon in a medium bowl. Set remaining ¾ cup of crumbs aside for cheesecake topping.

Press crumb mixture with hands or spoon into a 9-inch springform pan, lining bottom and sides of pan.

Chill crumb crust in refrigerator for approximately 1 hour.

Preheat oven to 325°.

Blend cream cheese with sugar, flour, and salt in a large bowl.

Separate eggs, set whites aside in a small bowl, and briskly stir yolks and vanilla into cheese mixture.

Stir heavy cream into cheese mixture, blending well.

Beat egg whites until stiff but not dry.

Fold into cheese mixture.

Pour cheese mixture into chilled crumb crust.

Sprinkle remaining ¾ cup of crumbs over top.

Bake for 1 to 1¼ hours, until center of cheesecake is set.

Turn off heat, open oven door, and let cheesecake stand for approximately 1 hour until cool.

Remove from springform pan.

Refrigerate cheesecake, lightly covered, for 8 to 12 hours before serving.

SERVING

Slice cheesecake and serve on small attractive plates.

Butterscotch Nine O'Clocks

INGREDIENTS

¾ cup all-purpose flour
¼ teaspoon baking powder
½ teaspoon salt
8 tablespoons (1 stick) butter
1 cup light brown sugar

2 eggs
1 teaspoon vanilla
¾ cup finely chopped nuts of your choice (pecans, walnuts, almonds, brazil nuts)

PREPARATION

Preheat oven to 350° at least 10 minutes before baking.

Butter an 8 × 8 × 2-inch baking pan.

Sift and measure ¾ cup of flour into a small bowl.

Sift again with baking powder and salt.

Melt butter in a medium saucepan over low heat.

Add brown sugar and stir with a wooden spoon until mixture is smooth.

Remove from heat and set aside to cool slightly.

Beat eggs into sugar mixture until well blended.

Beat in vanilla and flour until smooth.

Stir in chopped nuts.

Pour mixture into baking pan and spread evenly.

Bake for 20 to 25 minutes.

Remove from oven and set aside to cool.

SERVING

Cut into sixteen squares before serving on a decorative plate.

Note: Wrap leftover squares in foil to keep fresh.

Poor-Boy Brandied Peaches

INGREDIENTS

2 large fresh peaches, peeled,
  and cut into halves

1 tablespoon brown sugar

1 tablespoon butter, divided
  into four pats

4 sugar cubes

1 tablespoon brandy

PREPARATION

Wash and peel peaches.

Cut into halves and remove pit.

Place peach halves in a shallow baking dish.

Sprinkle brown sugar in hollow of each peach half and top with a small pat of butter.

Place baking dish under broiler.

Broil peaches for 3 to 5 minutes, or until brown sugar is crusty.

Soak sugar cubes in brandy.

Place a sugar cube on each peach half.

Drizzle any remaining brandy over peaches.

SERVING

Arrange peach halves in individual dessert bowls.

Light brandied sugar at the table, and flame peaches before serving.

Roquefort Cheese Mousse with Assorted Crackers

INGREDIENTS

5 ounces Roquefort cheese, grated

½ cup milk

1 cup heavy cream

PREPARATION

Chill a 2-cup mold to be used for the mousse.

Add cheese to milk in top of a double boiler over hot but not boiling water.

Stir until cheese is melted.

Set aside to cool.

Whip cream in a small bowl until thick enough to form a soft peak.

Fold whipped cream into cheese mixture.

Pour mixture into chilled mold.

Cover with foil.

Put a large attractive serving plate to be used in the refrigerator.

Chill cheese in the freezer until firm.

Remove from freezer and let cool water run over the mold.

SERVING

Unmold cheese mousse in the middle of chilled serving plate.

Arrange assorted crackers around the mousse.

Note: Use leftover mousse for snacking (preferably within 24 hours for taste and consistency).

After-Dinner Peppermint Wafers

INGREDIENTS

2 tablespoons (¼ stick) butter, softened

2 tablespoons corn oil

2 tablespoons warm water

Peppermint extract

2 cups confectioners' sugar, sifted and firmly packed

Food color (optional)

PREPARATION

Cream butter and corn oil in a medium bowl.

Add warm water and beat until light and creamy.

Stir in a few drops of peppermint extract to taste.

Sift and firmly pack 2 cups of confectioners' sugar.

Stir sugar gradually into butter mixture.

Blend well until mixture can be easily molded.

A few drops of food color of your choice may be added to the mixture if you prefer other than a white mint.

Peppermint mixture may be formed into small balls and flattened out on wax paper to make wafers, or shaped into a roll and sliced into wafers.

SERVING

Serve in a silver or other fancy candy dish.

Note: Recipe makes approximately 2 dozen peppermint wafers.

GREAT STEAKHOUSES OF THE UNITED STATES

ATLANTA
Coach and Six

BALTIMORE
The Prime Rib

BOSTON
Grill 23 & Bar
Hilltop Steak House (Saugus, MA)
Red Lion Inn (Cohasset, MA)

BUFFALO
McMahon's

CHICAGO
Arnie's
Gene and Georgetti's
Hy's
Morton's

DALLAS
Arthur's
The Hoffbrau Steak House
The Palm
Ruth's Chris Steakhouse

DETROIT
Carl's Chop House

DENVER
Emil-Lene's Sirloin House
The Buckhorn Exchange
The Colorado Mine Company
The Palm

D.C. (*Washington*)
J.R.'s Stockyards Inn (Tyson Corners, VA)
Morton's of Chicago
The Palm
The Prime Rib

FORT WORTH
Hoffbrau Steaks of Fort Worth

HOUSTON
Brenner's Steak House
Bud Bigelow's Charcoal House
The Palm

INDIANAPOLIS
St. Elmo's

KANSAS CITY
Golden Ox Restaurant
Hereford House

LOS ANGELES
Marcus Steak House
Pacific Dining Car
The Palm

LOUISVILLE
The Fifth Quarter

MIAMI
Christy's
Old Forge
The Palm

MINNEAPOLIS
Murray's Restaurant

NEW ORLEANS
 Chris's

NEW YORK CITY
 Christ Cella
 Frank's on 14th Street
 Peter Luger Steak House (Brooklyn, NY)
 Sparks Steak House
 The Palm

PHILADELPHIA
 Arthur's Steak House
 The Blue Bird (Clairton, PA)

SAN FRANCISCO
 Alfred's
 Harris's

TAMPA
 Bern's Steak House

WILMINGTON
 Constantineau's House of Beef

INDEX